CHILDREN'S ENCYCLOPEDIA
OF ROCKS AND FOSSILS

Claudia Martin

ARCTURUS

ARCTURUS

This edition published in 2019 by Arcturus Publishing Limited
26/27 Bickels Yard, 151–153 Bermondsey Street,
London SE1 3HA

Consultant: Chris Jarvis
Author and Editor: Claudia Martin
Designer: Amy McSimpson @ Hollow Pond

Copyright © Arcturus Holdings Limited

ISBN: 978-1-78950-595-5
CH006563US
Supplier 29, Date 0519, Print run 8121

Printed in China

In this book, one billion means one thousand million (1,000,000,000) and one trillion means one million million (1,000,000,000,000).

CHILDREN'S ENCYCLOPEDIA OF ROCKS AND FOSSILS

CONTENTS

Rocky Planet

The outer layers of our planet are rock. Beneath city streets, grass, forests, and oceans is rock of many different types, hiding many different treasures. Rock may be hard, soft, crumbly, or shiny. What is certain is that rock is more changeable and surprising than most people ever imagine.

Beautiful Planet

Shaped by volcanoes, earth movements, wind, water, and ice, rock has made our planet a beautiful and sometimes challenging playground. Rock gives us mountains to climb, deserts to hike across, and beaches to play on.

Rock Art

Around 3.3 million years ago, our ancestors learned how to shape rock into simple tools. It was not until 40,000 years ago that humans had the time, skill, and imagination to carve rock into art. Since then, artists and craftspeople have cut, ground, or polished rock to make artworks from statues to gravestones.

These Buddhist monks are making a mandala out of grains of rock that are dyed different shades. A mandala is a pattern that represents the whole Universe.

Rock Construction

For thousands of years, slabs and bricks of rock have been used to construct homes, temples, and meeting places. Rock tiles cover roofs and floors. Ground into gravel or sand, rock is also an ingredient in road-building and cement, which sets hard to stick other materials together.

Around 4,500 years ago, slabs of limestone and granite rock were used to construct the pyramids at Giza, in Egypt, as tombs for pharaohs.

DID YOU KNOW? The world's oldest building is a rock tomb, in Barnénez, France, constructed around 6,800 years ago to house the dead.

Gemstones

Since the days when humans first settled in villages and towns, people have wondered at the glittering gemstones that can be found hidden in rocks. Miners have risked their lives to dig gems from deep underground, or searched through gravel in riverbeds. Traders have carried gems far and wide. Today, our love of gemstones is as great as ever.

The Imperial State Crown is owned by the kings and queens of the United Kingdom. This red gemstone is not a ruby, but a spinel.

This reddish rock is sandstone, while the valley floor is siltstone.

Monument Valley, in the southwestern United States, is famous for its amazingly shaped rocks.

Fossils

Fossils are some of the greatest treasures to be found in rocks. These hardened remains of ancient animals and plants can teach us what our planet was like long ago. Fossils show us fierce dinosaurs, gentle mammoths, and our own ancestors.

Gryposaurus was a duckbilled dinosaur that lived 83–74 million years ago.

The Earth

The Earth is a rocky ball, with a super-hot core of metal. Geology is the study of the rocks and other materials that form our planet. Geologists study how the Earth was made—and how its rocks carry on changing in amazing and beautiful ways.

Formation of the Earth

Our planet formed about 4.54 billion years ago in the cloud of gas and dust left over from the formation of the new Sun. Pulled by gravity, the gas and dust started to form clumps, which slowly grew into planets. The four planets nearest the Sun—Mercury, Venus, Earth, and Mars—formed from metal and rocky materials. The colder, outer planets—Jupiter, Saturn, Uranus, and Neptune—are mostly ices and gases.

At first, the super-hot Earth was molten and constantly battered by space rocks. Slowly, the Earth's surface cooled, hardening into solid rock. About 3.8 billion years ago, Earth had cooled enough for rain to fall, filling the basins that are now our oceans.

Land covers 29 percent of Earth's surface. The thick crust that forms the Earth's continents is called the continental crust.

Earth's Structure

The Earth's crust is solid rock. Beneath the crust, the mantle is made of rocks that are hot enough to partly melt and to flow very slowly. Earth's core is made mostly of the metals iron and nickel. The outer core is liquid, while the inner core is under so much pressure it is a solid ball.

1. **Crust:** Gets hotter with depth, up to 400°C (750°F)
2. **Mantle:** 500-4,000°C (900-7,200°F)
3. **Outer core:** 4,000-6,000°C (7,200-10,800°F)
4. **Inner core:** Around 6,000°C (10,800°F)

DID YOU KNOW? The Moon formed about 4.51 billion years ago, probably from the rocks thrown out by a collision between Earth and a Mars-sized planet.

The crust beneath the oceans is called the oceanic crust. It is thinner than the continental crust, usually less than 10 km (6 miles) thick.

Around 71 percent of Earth's surface is covered by seas and oceans.

PLANET EARTH FACTS

Radius of Earth (distance from surface to middle): 6,378 km (3,963 miles)

Depth of crust: 5–70 km (3–43 miles)

Depth of mantle: Down to 2,890 km (1,796 miles)

Depth of outer core: Down to 5,160 km (3,206 miles)

Radius of inner core: Around 1,218 km (757 miles)

Earth

Elements

Everything on Earth—from rocks and metals to people and plants—is made of one or more elements. Elements are the simplest possible substances, which means that they cannot be broken down into other substances.

Atoms and Elements

Each element is made of its own type of atom. Atoms are tiny particles, about a ten-billionth of a meter across. There are 118 known elements, so there are also 118 known types of atoms. Around 90 of the elements are metals, such as gold, iron, and aluminum. Metals are usually solid and shiny at room temperature. Many of the other, non-metal elements are gases at room temperature, such as oxygen and hydrogen. A few of the other elements are also solid at room temperature, such as silicon and carbon.

The most common compound on Earth is water. Each molecule (or group of joined atoms) in water contains one oxygen atom and two hydrogen atoms.

This is silicon, a very common element in Earth's crust. Around 90 percent of rocks in the crust contain silicon.

Made entirely of the element aluminum, this statue is in Piccadilly Circus, London. It contains trillions and trillions of aluminum atoms!

Oxygen: 47 percent

Silicon: 28 percent

Aluminum: 8 percent

Iron: 5 percent

Calcium, sodium, potassium, magnesium, and others: 12 percent

Mining iron from Earth's crust

Strange as it seems, the most common element in the rocks of Earth's crust is oxygen—the gas that we breathe. This is because oxygen easily forms compounds with other elements.

Compounds and Minerals

Elements often combine to form compounds. A compound is made of atoms of different elements that are bonded to each other. Compounds can be liquids, such as water (containing hydrogen and oxygen); gases, such as carbon dioxide (containing carbon and oxygen); or solids, such as salt (containing sodium and chlorine). A solid compound that forms naturally is called a mineral.

The mineral kyanite is a compound containing atoms of silicon, aluminum, and oxygen. Kyanite forms in Earth's crust.

DID YOU KNOW? The most common element in the human body is oxygen, which makes up 65 percent of us!

Rocks

Rocks can be hard or crumbly, brown or pink, striped or speckled. So what are rocks? All rocks are solid mixtures of different minerals. Different types of rocks contain different minerals. The most common rocks are made of common minerals, which contain common elements.

Grains in Granite

The common rock granite contains the minerals feldspar and quartz, with smaller amounts of mica or hornblende. These are common minerals, which all contain the elements silicon and oxygen, alongside aluminum, calcium, and others.

In Torres del Paine National Park, Chile, are the peaks known as Los Cuernos ("The Horns"). This paler rock is granite.

Granite is named for its grainy texture. Large grains of the dark minerals mica and hornblende can be seen among the paler feldspar and quartz.

This is a chunk of feldspar, the most common mineral in Earth's crust.

Feldspar

The mineral feldspar makes up around half of Earth's crust. Geologists call it a common "rock-forming mineral." As well as being found in granite, feldspar is in many other rocks, such as basalt, gneiss, gabbro, and diorite.

MOST COMMON ROCKS IN THE CRUST

Basalt and gabbro: 43 percent

Gneiss: 21 percent

Diorite and granodiorite: 11 percent

Granite: 10 percent

Schist: 5 percent

Others: 10 percent

Zuma Rock, Nigeria, a giant chunk of gabbro

The jagged, dark summits are shale rock, which is made of hardened mud.

Most of the crust is covered by ocean, soil and plants, or cities, but rock is often exposed on high mountains and steep cliffs. These are great places to study rocks.

DID YOU KNOW? Geologists name at least 130 rock types, all with different mineral mixtures, textures, and ways of forming.

Moving Plates

The Earth's crust is not one unbroken chunk of rock. Together with the upper part of the mantle, it is broken into several giant pieces. These are called tectonic plates. The plates move very, very slowly, driven by movements in the super-hot rock of the mantle.

Plate Boundaries

The edges of the plates are called boundaries. As the plates move against—or apart from—each other, they shape the surface of our planet. Without moving plates, the Earth's surface would be almost featureless, with no mountains or volcanoes. Most volcanoes and earthquakes occur at the edges of plates.

In 2010, a massive earthquake shook Haiti in the Caribbean. It was caused by movement between the major North American and the smaller Caribbean plates.

TYPES OF BOUNDARIES

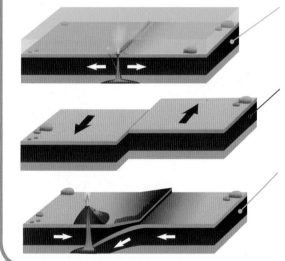

DIVERGENT BOUNDARY
A divergent boundary is where two plates are moving apart. Melted rock from the mantle, called magma, rises up to fill the space. Deep valleys, called rifts, can be created.

TRANSFORM BOUNDARY
A transform boundary is where two plates are grinding past each other. When the rocks get stuck against each other, then break and slip past, the result is a strong earthquake.

CONVERGENT BOUNDARY
When two plates are moving toward each other, mountain ranges can form as rock is pushed upward. As one plate slides beneath the other, magma can be forced up, forming volcanoes.

MOST POWERFUL EARTHQUAKES

Rated on the moment magnitude scale

Valdivia, Chile, 1960: 9.4–9.6 (1,000–7,000 killed)

Prince William Sound, Alaska, USA, 1964: 9.2 (139 killed)

Indian Ocean, near Sumatra, Indonesia, 2004: 9.1–9.3 (227,898 killed)

Pacific Ocean, near Tohoku, Japan, 2011: 9.1 (15,896 killed)

Kamchatka, Russia, 1952: 9.0 (2,336 killed)

The 1960 Valdivia Earthquake

A Jigsaw of Plates

There are eight large plates and several smaller ones. Over millions of years, the movement of the plates has formed and broken up our land masses. Around 3.6 billion years ago, all the Earth's land was one giant continent, called a supercontinent. This broke up into separate continents, then new supercontinents formed and broke up, as many as 10 times!

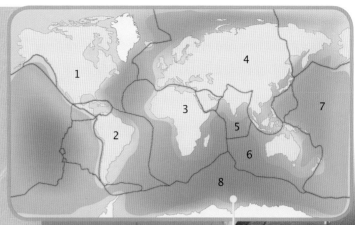

KEY

1. North American Plate
2. South American Plate
3. African Plate
4. Eurasian Plate
5. Indian Plate
6. Australian Plate
7. Pacific Plate
8. Antarctic Plate

As the ground shook, more than 250,000 homes collapsed, as well as schools, hospitals, roads, and phone lines.

Rescuers hunt for people who may be trapped in the rubble.

DID YOU KNOW? Tectonic plates move, on average, about 3 cm (1.2 inches) per year, or around 30 km (19 miles) over 1 million years.

13

Mountains

A mountain is a large peak of rock that rises above the surrounding land. Some mountains stand alone, but most are part of mountain ranges, where a series of mountains are in a line or curve. There are also mountains and mountain ranges beneath the sea: some islands are actually the tops of mountains.

Fold and Fault-Block Mountains

There are three types of mountains: fold mountains, fault-block mountains, and volcanoes (see page 16). All mountains take millions of years to form. Fold and fault-block mountains are made by the movement of Earth's plates.

MOUNTAIN BUILDING

 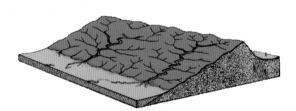

FOLD MOUNTAINS
Fold mountains form at convergent plate boundaries. As the plates move toward each other, rock is pushed and folded upward like a rumpled tablecloth.

FAULT–BLOCK MOUNTAINS
Fault-block mountains form where the rock is broken into chunks by plate movement. Some chunks are forced upward, sometimes on a tilt, and others are forced down.

LONGEST MOUNTAIN RANGE ON EACH CONTINENT

South America: Andes, 7,240 km (4,500 miles)
Africa: Southern Great Escarpment, 5,000 km (3,100 miles)
North America: Rocky Mountains, 4,800 km (3,000 miles)
Antarctica: Transantarctic Mountains, 3,540 km (2,200 miles)
Australia: Great Dividing Range, 3,500 km (2,175 miles)
Asia: Himalayas, 2,400 km (1,500 miles)
Europe: Scandinavian Mountains, 1,700 km (1,100 miles)

Scandinavian Mountains

The Sierra Nevada

The Sierra Nevada range, in the western United States, are fault-block mountains. About 5 million years ago, a block of crust started to lift and tilt as a smaller plate moved beneath the North American Plate. The lifting and tilting continues today, sometimes causing earthquakes in the region.

The Himalaya mountains, in Asia, are fold mountains. The range started to form about 50 million years ago as the Indian Plate slid under the Eurasian Plate.

Along the eastern edge of the Sierra Nevada mountains, we can see the nearly straight edge of the uptilted block of crust.

Climbers come from all over the world to test their skills on one of the range's 50 mountains that are over 7,200 m (23,600 ft) tall.

DID YOU KNOW? The longest mountain range of all is beneath the Atlantic Ocean: the Mid-Ocean Ridge is about 16,000 km (10,000 miles) long.

Volcanoes

A volcano is a hole or crack in the crust which lets melted rock escape. Volcanoes are often found where tectonic plates are moving together or apart, melting rock and forcing it to the surface. However, some volcanoes form in the middle of plates, over "hotspots" in the mantle.

Eruptions

Volcanoes are above a magma chamber, a pool of melted rock. When this magma is put under enough pressure, it rushes to the surface in an eruption, along with hot gas and ash. When it has erupted, magma is called lava. Volcanoes often grow into mountains as lava cools and hardens, building up in one eruption after another.

VOLCANO TYPES

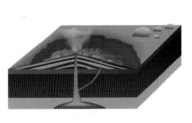

FISSURE VENT
This is a long crack in the crust, through which lava can flow. Eruptions from fissure vents do not usually build tall mountains of cooled lava.

SHIELD VOLCANO
This type of volcano is named for its flattened shape, like a warrior's shield, which is made from the build-up of runny lava that flows a distance before hardening.

STRATOVOLCANO
A stratovolcano has a steep cone shape made from layers of thick lava, rocks, and ash. Eruptions are more likely to be explosive, throwing material high into the air.

MOST ACTIVE VOLCANOES

All erupting almost continually

Kilauea, Hawaiian Islands, USA: Shield volcano, 1,247 m (4,09

Mount Etna, Italy: Stratovolcano, 3,329 m (10,922 ft)

Stromboli, Italy: Stratovolcano, 924 m (3,031 ft)

Mount Yasur, Vanuatu: Stratovolcano, 361 m (1,184 ft)

Sangay, Ecuador: Stratovolcano, 5,300 m (17,400 ft)

Lava flow from Kilauea

Active, Dormant, and Extinct

A volcano that is likely to erupt at some point is called "active." A volcano that has not erupted in a very long time is "dormant." An "extinct" volcano no longer has a supply of magma beneath it, so it cannot erupt again.

1. Mount Fuji, in Japan, is a stratovolcano. It has not erupted since 1707, but geologists do not agree on whether to call it active or dormant.

2. Piton de la Fournaise, on Réunion Island in the Indian Ocean, is a highly active shield volcano.

Although Etna erupts frequently, only 77 people are known to have been killed since 1500 BCE. The volcano's lava flows quite slowly, giving people time to evacuate.

Etna gets its name from the ancient Greek word *aitho*, which means "I burn."

DID YOU KNOW? The Hawaiian Islands, in the Pacific Ocean, are the exposed summits of 17 major volcanoes that formed over a hotspot.

17

The Rock Cycle

Earth's rocks are always changing, although they do it very slowly—over thousands or millions of years! There are three groups of rocks, each formed in a different way: igneous, sedimentary, and metamorphic. The "rock cycle" is the ways that rocks are altered or destroyed—changing from one group of rocks to another.

Rock Groups

Igneous rocks form when magma or lava cools and hardens into solid rock. Sedimentary rocks are mades when bits of rock, minerals, plants, or animal skeletons are pressed together for millions of years, slowly hardening into rock. Metamorphic rocks are formed in the crust when any rock is put under great heat or pressure, bringing about changes in its make-up. These rock-making processes are always going on, driven by the movement of Earth's tectonic plates as well as by the erosion, or wearing away, done by water, wind, and ice.

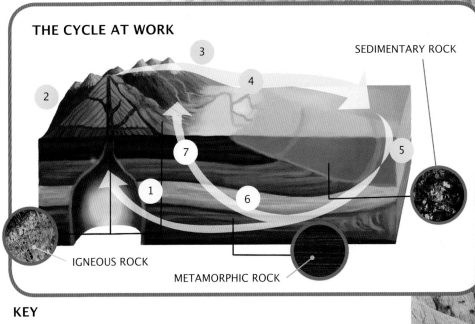

THE CYCLE AT WORK

SEDIMENTARY ROCK

IGNEOUS ROCK

METAMORPHIC ROCK

KEY

1. Rock melts into magma, then hardens into igneous rock.

2. Other magma erupts as lava from a volcano, then cools into igneous rock.

3. At the surface, rock is battered by weather and eroded.

4. Bits of rock and mineral, called sediment, are transported by rivers and rain.

5. Sediment is buried, hardening into sedimentary rock.

6. Movement of tectonic plates creates pressure and heat, forming metamorphic rock.

7. Rock is lifted to the surface by movement of the plates.

ROCK CYCLE RECORDS

Fastest tectonic plate: Tonga Plate, 24 cm (9.4 in) per year

Fastest growing mountain: Nanga Parbat, in the Himalayas, 7 mm (0.3 in) per year

Fastest eroding coast: Holderness, UK, 2 m (6.6 ft) per year

Fastest eroding mountains: Southern Alps, New Zealand, 2.5 mm (0.1 in) per year

Nanga Parbat

DID YOU KNOW? Sedimentary rocks cover three-quarters of the surface of Earth's land, although they make up less than one-tenth of the weight of the whole crust.

The Rock Cycle on Mars

Like Earth, Mars has a metal core and a rocky mantle and crust. Mars also has igneous, metamorphic, and sedimentary rocks. Mars's rock cycle is not currently very active, because it does not have moving tectonic plates and no flowing water on its surface. However, studying Mars's rocks has led scientists to think that, long ago, Mars had erupting volcanoes, flowing oceans, and falling rain.

This photograph of Mars's rocky surface was taken by the *Sojourner* rover, a robotic vehicle that explored the planet in 1997.

In Badlands National Park, USA, erosion by rivers, rain, and wind has worn the rock into buttes (isolated hills) and pinnacles (columns of rock).

The stripes are layers of different sedimentary rocks, formed at different times by volcanic ash, sand, and mud.

The Work of Water

Water plays a huge part in the rock cycle through weathering and erosion. Rainwater weathers, or breaks down, rock by dissolving or crumbling it. Rivers and seas carry away these fragments in a process called erosion.

Beaches

Beaches are found along coasts and other bodies of water. They are made by waves eroding cliffs, as well as coral reefs and rocks offshore. The bits of broken rock, which may be sand-sized or pebbles, are carried along and then deposited, or left behind, by waves and currents.

Over millions of years, the San Juan River, in Utah, USA, has eroded a winding canyon through the rock.

This is a sandspit, a ridge of sand stretching into the sea from a beach. It is made by waves carrying sand along the coast, then dropping it where the coastline turns a corner.

Praia do Cassino

COASTAL RECORDS

Longest beach: Praia do Cassino, Brazil, 245 km (152 miles)

Longest manmade beach: Biloxi-Gulfport, USA, 42 km (26 miles)

Longest sandspit: Arabat Spit, Ukraine, 112 km (70 miles)

Tallest sea cliffs: Kalaupapa Cliffs, Hawaii, 1,010 m (3,315 ft) high

Longest sea cave: Matanaka Cave, New Zealand, 1,500 m (4,920 ft)

Sea Caves

Caves can form in coasts because of erosion by waves. Waves are constantly wearing away cliffs, but caves are made where there is a crack or weakness in the rock, quickening the erosion in that spot.

The erosion of a cave is speeded up by rough sand and pebbles being tossed around by the waves.

Bends in a river are called meanders. They form because rivers erode rock and soil from the outer curve of their path, then deposit it on an inner curve a little downstream. This makes meanders grow larger and larger.

These very tight meanders are called goosenecks, because they are like the curved neck of a goose!

DID YOU KNOW? Pfeiffer Beach, in the United States, is famous for its purple sand, which contains fragments of the mineral garnet.

More Erosion

Other forces play their part in weathering and eroding rocks, including ice, wind, and even plants and animals. Plant roots grow through cracks in rock, then break it apart as they grow. Animals from shellfish to tiny bacteria wear away rock by burrowing or making chemicals that dissolve it.

Ice

Water can seep into rocks. When the temperature drops, the water freezes into ice, which makes it expand. This can slowly break rock apart. Glaciers are rivers of ice made from packed-together snow. They are common on high mountains, where they slide down valleys at speeds of up to a few meters per day. Rocks get stuck in the bottom of the glacier and carried along with it. As they move, the rocks grind down the rock beneath, wearing away U-shaped valleys.

Strong winds blew loose particles away from the sandstone, then this loose sand rubbed away at the rock walls.

This valley in Europe's Alps mountains was eroded during the last ice age, when temperatures were much colder than now. Northern Europe was covered by glaciers, shaping the landscapes we see today.

This landform in Arizona, USA, is called The Wave. These troughs were first eroded by rainwater, then shaped by wind.

DID YOU KNOW? Humans cause soil erosion when we cut down forests, leaving the soil exposed to wind and rain.

Tallest dune: Dune 7, Namibia, 383 m (1,256 ft)

Fastest-moving dunes: Bodélé Depression, Sahara Desert, Chad, dunes move between 10 m (33 ft) and 70 m (230 m) per year

Largest erg (sandy desert): Rub' al Khali, Arabian Peninsula, 650,000 sq km (251,000 sq miles)

Dune 7

Gravity

Everything on Earth is pulled downward by gravity! Soil is a mixture of minerals from nearby rocks, the remains of dead plants and animals, and water. Very slowly, it creeps downhill. This process can be speeded up by heavy rainfall, which can cause mudslides. Loose rocks can fall suddenly downhill in rockfalls. Soft rocks, such as clay and mudstone, can slip downhill after rain.

The ridged ripples are made by softer and harder layers in the sandstone. Harder layers erode more slowly.

After rockfalls, broken chunks of rock collect at the bottom of mountains and cliffs. These fragments are called scree.

Useful Rocks

We cut rocks and minerals from the ground in open pits, or excavate them from mines tunnelled into the crust. Some rocks and minerals are used as construction materials, while others find their way into factories, scientists' laboratories, farms, or artists' workshops.

Mining Minerals

Dozens of different elements and minerals are mined around the world, from glittering metals and precious gems to minerals that look dull but are extremely useful. Among the most commonly mined minerals is feldspar, which is used as an ingredient in glass, pottery, soaps, and glues. Gypsum is used as a fertilizer to feed crops, and as an ingredient in plaster and cement.

The Super Pit open-pit gold mine is in Kalgoorlie, Australia.

This halite mine is in Germany. Halite is also known as rock salt. It is used in food and to make leather, soap, printed photographs, and scientific equipment.

MINE RECORDS

Oldest mine: Ngwenya, Swaziland, red ocher and iron, 41,000–43,000 years old

Deepest mine: Mponeng, South Africa, gold, 4 km (2.5 miles) deep

Largest open-pit mine: Bingham Canyon, USA, copper, 4 km (2.5 miles) wide and 1.2 km (0.75 miles) deep

Most valuable mine: Cigar Lake, Canada, uranium, produces 7,850 tonnes (8,650 tons) per year

Ngwenya Mine

The pit is 3.5 km (2.2 miles) long, 1.5 km (0.9 miles) wide, and 700 m (2,300 ft) deep. About 28 tonnes (31 tons) of gold is dug out every year.

Discovering the Past

Rocks are a window into the past! Sedimentary rocks often form in layers, with the oldest layers at the bottom. Through studying rock layers all around the world, scientists can determine how old each layer is. This means that, when the fossil of an ancient animal or plant is found in a layer of rock, scientists can tell how long ago it lived.

Layers of rock are called strata. The study of those layers is called stratigraphy.

Rock containing flakes and chunks of gold is removed using drills and explosives, then carried away in trucks.

DID YOU KNOW? The mineral fluorite is put in toothpaste as a source of fluorine, which protects against tooth decay.

Making Igneous Rocks

Igneous rock is made when melted rock cools and hardens into solid rock. Melted rock, or magma, is found in Earth's mantle and crust. The oldest igneous rocks are almost 4 billion years old, while new igneous rocks are constantly forming around active volcanoes.

Intrusive and Extrusive

There are two types of igneous rocks: intrusive (meaning "flowing inside") and extrusive (meaning "forced out"). When magma cools and hardens inside the Earth, it becomes intrusive igneous rock. If magma is forced up to the surface through a volcano, it is called lava. When lava cools down, it hardens into extrusive igneous rock.

IGNEOUS FORMATIONS

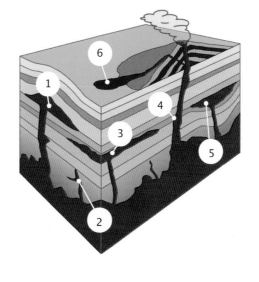

1. Magma squeezes up between layers of rock and then cools, forming a dome of intrusive igneous rock called a "laccolith."

2. Magma flows into a vertical crack, making a "dyke" of intrusive igneous rock.

3. A sheet of intrusive igneous rock is a "sill."

4. A "plug" of intrusive igneous rock is made when magma cools inside the vent of a volcano.

5. An upside-down dome is called a "lopolith."

6. Cooled lava forms extrusive igneous rock.

IGNEOUS ROCK TEXTURES

Glassy: Extrusive rocks that cooled too quickly for crystals to form
Aphanitic: Extrusive rocks with grains too small to be seen
Pyroclastic: Extrusive rocks made of fragments thrown from a volcano
Porphyritic: Intrusive or extrusive rocks with large crystals among fine grains
Phaneritic: Intrusive rocks with grains large enough to be seen with the naked eye
Pegmatitic: Intrusive rocks with massive crystals

Larvikite, a phaneritic rock

Devil's Tower in Wyoming, USA, probably formed 40 million years ago when magma cooled inside a volcano, creating a plug of an intrusive igneous rock called phonolite.

The softer rock surrounding the plug has eroded, leaving behind the phonolite.

Cooling Fast or Slow

Extrusive igneous rock is exposed to the air or seawater, so it cools much more quickly than intrusive rock. This means that its texture is different. As intrusive rock slowly cools, its minerals have time to grow into crystals, in which the atoms have formed a neat and orderly structure. We can see crystals as grains or even as big lumps. Extrusive rock has no time to form large crystals. Sometimes it cools so fast that it has a shiny, glassy texture.

Cooled lava has formed basalt, an extrusive igneous rock, at Hawaii Volcanoes National Park.

DID YOU KNOW? "Igneous" comes from the Latin word *ignis*, meaning "fire." Magma usually has a temperature of 700–1,300°C (1,300–2,400°F).

Granite

Granite is a very common intrusive igneous rock. It is formed as magma cools slowly beneath Earth's surface, growing large grains of pale quartz and feldspar minerals, alongside speckles of darker minerals.

A Hard Rock

Granite is exposed at the Earth's surface where it has been pushed upward by plate movement and the softer, sedimentary rocks that covered it have been eroded. Granite is a very hard rock that erodes more slowly than other rocks. It often forms features called tors, which are chunks of rock that stand alone.

This tor is in Dartmoor, England. The joints in the rocks are caused by weathering and erosion.

Machu Picchu

Granite's toughness has made it useful as a construction stone for thousands of years. The Inca city of Machu Picchu, in Peru, was built in the 15th century from granite that was quarried from the surrounding mountains.

The homes, temples, and warehouses in Machu Picchu are made from carefully carved blocks of granite, fitted tightly without any mortar to stick them together.

GRANITE

Formation: Intrusive

Texture: Phaneritic

Appearance: White, gray, or pink with darker grains

Properties: Hard, slow to erode, and easy to polish

Minerals: Largely quartz and feldspar, plus mica, hornblende, and others

Granite

The mountains of Huangshan, China, are often called the "Sea of Clouds" because they look like islands above the mist.

The granite that forms the mountains was lifted to the surface 100 million years ago, then eroded into jagged peaks by glaciers.

Pines cling to rocky ledges where they can find enough soil to take root.

DID YOU KNOW? Sculptors Gutzon and Lincoln Borglum carved the faces of four US presidents from a granite cliff on Mount Rushmore, USA.

29

Diorite

This intrusive igneous rock is quite rare. Diorite is an extremely hard rock, which makes it difficult to cut or sculpt. However, when stone carvers are skilled enough to work with it, the buildings, sculptures, and weapons they make are very long-lasting.

Carving Out History

Diorite was popular for statues and inscriptions (writing carved into stone) in the ancient civilizations of the Middle East, including Egypt, Babylonia, and Assyria. The famous Code of Hammurabi is a list of laws that was carved into a block of diorite on the orders of the Babylonian king Hammurabi in about 1754 BCE.

Gudea had many statues of himself placed in temples throughout his land.

The Code of Hammurabi contains 282 laws and their punishments, carved in cuneiform script, one of the earliest systems of writing. The symbols represent sounds or whole words.

DID YOU KNOW? The Middle Eastern king Sargon of Akkad (around 2334–2284 BCE) ordered his soldiers to bring back diorite when they invaded other lands.

DIORITE

Formation: Intrusive

Texture: Phaneritic or porphyritic

Appearance: Gray to black, with white speckles or orbs

Properties: Extremely hard, but can be finely carved and polished

Minerals: Feldspar, hornblende, biotite, and pyroxene

Diorite with orbs

This statue of Gudea, ruler of ancient Lagash (in modern Iraq), was carved from diorite in around 2120 BCE.

There was no source of diorite in Lagash, so the stone was brought from hundreds of miles away.

Melting and Mixing

The plates that form the continents contain a lot of granite, while the oceanic plates that make the seafloor are largely basalt (see page 34). Diorite is usually formed where an oceanic plate is moving under a continental plate. Melted basalt rises, mixes a little with the granite, and slowly cools to form diorite. For this reason, diorite can often be spotted around granite.

The "North America Wall" in Yosemite National Park, USA, is named for the darker North America–shaped splodge of diorite in the granite cliff.

Dunite

Dunite is a common rock right down inside the mantle, but it is not often spotted at Earth's surface. However, this intrusive rock can form in the crust where plates are moving toward each other, forcing up magma from deep underground.

Valuable Rock

Dunite and similar mantle rocks contain the mineral chromite. Chromite contains the metals chromium and iron, as well as oxygen. The mineral is often mined, then processed to extract the chromium. Chromium is very useful, as it is slow to tarnish. Tarnishing is when metal gets a dark coating when exposed to air.

Chromium can be used as a tarnish–resistant coating, called chrome plating, on other metals. The metal parts of cars and motorbikes are often chrome plated.

Twin Sisters Mountain, in Washington State, USA, is formed from dunite that has been thrust to the surface.

DID YOU KNOW? Dunite is named after Dun Mountain, in New Zealand, which is itself named for its dun (reddish brown) shade.

Green to Brown

About 90 percent of dunite is the mineral olivine, which is named for its olive green color. A large, perfect crystal of olivine is considered a gemstone and given the name peridot. Although dunite rock often has a greenish tint, it can turn reddish brown when exposed to air. This is because olivine contains iron, which rusts in damp air.

At 2,025 m (6,644 ft), North Twin is the lower of the twin peaks. South Twin (to the left) is 110 m (360 ft) higher.

Peridot is a gemstone that forms in dunite and other rocks that contain lots of the elements magnesium and iron.

DUNITE

Formation: Intrusive

Texture: Phaneritic

Appearance: Greenish–gray, often turning brown when exposed to air

Properties: Hard, rough, and contains useful minerals

Minerals: Mostly olivine, plus chromite, magnetite, and others

Dunite

Basalt

The most common igneous rock, basalt forms from the quick cooling of lava that has erupted from a volcano or surged up where two plates are moving apart on the seafloor. Basalt lava contains lots of magnesium and iron. This sort of lava is very runny, so it covers wide areas before hardening.

Making Pillows

When basalt lava erupts under water, it can form pillow-like shapes. When the hot lava touches the water, the surface of the lava cools quickly. More lava flows into the "tongue" of hardened lava, blowing it up like a balloon. Eventually the build-up of lava breaks the hard skin, then a new pillow of lava starts to form.

These 580-million-year-old basalt pillows are on the beach of Anglesey, Wales. They were once on the ocean floor.

The Giant's Causeway, in Northern Ireland, is made up of 40,000 basalt columns.

Forming Columns

As a thick flow of lava cools in the air, cracks form as it hardens and shrinks. These cracks grow and spread until they make a regular pattern, often forming hexagonal columns.

The Svartifoss waterfall, in Iceland, flows over basalt columns.

BASALT

Formation: Extrusive

Texture: Aphanitic or porphyritic

Appearance: Gray to black, but can turn rust brown in air

Properties: Hard and tough

Minerals: Feldspar, pyroxene, and olivine

Basalt

The columns formed 50-60 million years ago as lava cooled and cracked following a massive eruption from a fissure vent.

Most of the columns are hexagonal, or six-sided, but some have four, five, seven, or eight sides.

DID YOU KNOW? Basalt is also common on the Moon, where it forms the dark "seas" we can see from Earth.

Obsidian

The extrusive rock obsidian is formed when lava cools so fast that no mineral crystals can grow at all. This gives it a smooth, glass-like texture. Obsidian is found at the edges of lava flows that also form rhyolite (see page 44), which contains the same elements but cools more slowly.

Sharp Edges

Since obsidian does not contain interlocking crystals, it is quite easy to break—and breaks along smooth, straight lines. This means its edges can be very sharp—and useful! Obsidian tools have been used for slicing and piercing since the Stone Age.

Brennisteinsalda volcano, in Iceland, is made of layers of rhyolite.

Obsidian tools, called *mata'a*, were used for hundreds of years on Easter Island, off Chile, for cutting, scraping, and planting.

Obsidian

OBSIDIAN

Formation: Extrusive

Texture: Glassy

Appearance: Usually black

Properties: Hard, smooth, and breaks with sharp edges

Minerals: Hornblende, feldspar, quartz, biotite, and others

DID YOU KNOW? Today, some surgeons use obsidian blades during operations, as the rock can cut more finely than even the metal steel.

The volcano's bright colors are made by elements such as sulfur (yellow) and iron (red).

At the edges of the rhyolite flow, faster-cooling lava has formed obsidian boulders.

Apache Tears

Pebbles of obsidian, called "Apache tears," are found in the southwestern United States. They get their name from a legend about a band of Apache Native American warriors, who rode their horses over a cliff rather than be killed by US government soldiers. The tears of the warriors' wives and children were said to turn to stone as they hit the ground.

Apache tears are bubbles of obsidian that form inside lava flows.

Pumice

Pumice is formed when lava is thrown violently from a volcano. The frothy lava cools very rapidly, creating pumice's bubbly texture. As pumice is full of holes, it is lightweight and can even float on water.

Put to Good Use

Since pumice is lightweight, it can be used to bind together concrete and plaster for structures that need to be light, such as domes and bridges. Pumice is also abrasive, which means it rubs away other materials. The rock is used in polishes and to manufacture "stone-washed," or fashionably worn-looking, jeans. Since pumice is porous, which means it lets water pass through, it is also used to filter dirt and germs from drinking water.

The Campo de Piedra Pómez ("Pumice Stone Field"), in Argentina, is a desert covered with a layer of pumice.

Pumice is used to rub away the hard skin on feet. These "pumice stones" have been dyed.

PUMICE

Formation: Extrusive

Texture: Pyroclastic

Appearance: Usually pale, from white to brown

Properties: Lightweight, porous, and abrasive

Minerals: Depends on the lava type, but often feldspar, augite, hornblende, and zircon

Pumice

DID YOU KNOW? When they clean your teeth, dentists use a pumice mixture to rub away the plaque, which is a sticky film caused by bacteria.

Igneous Island

The Greek island Gyali is part of an underwater volcano and is made of the extrusive igneous rocks pumice, rhyolite, and obsidian. Gyali, which means glass in Greek, is named after its glassy obsidian. The pumice is cut from huge quarries, occupying about a quarter of the island.

The Carachi Pampa volcano is one of many in the area caused by the Nazca Plate moving under western Southern America.

Pumice from Gyali's quarries is transported around the world for use in construction.

The pumice has been eroded into strange shapes by the wind, which whips around rough flakes of pumice.

Tuff

Tuff is a rock formed from the ash thrown out of a volcano. Volcanic ash is made of tiny pieces of rocks and minerals that are ground up in an explosive eruption. Tuff can contain a range of different minerals, depending on the volcano.

Moai

Between around 1250 and 1500 CE, the inhabitants of Easter Island, in the Pacific Ocean, carved blocks of tuff and other igneous rocks into giant human figures, called *moai*. These statues represent the sculptors' ancestors, watching over the living.

Tuff is suitable for carving *moai* because it is quite soft and lightweight, making it easy to shape and transport.

In central Turkey, there are many tall spires of tuff, called "fairy chimneys."

Tuff

TUFF

Formation: Extrusive

Texture: Pyroclastic

Appearance: Depends on the volcano

Properties: Soft, rough, and porous

Minerals: Depends on the volcano, but may contain leucite, augite, and olivine

The area was once covered by a thick layer of tuff, with a coating of basalt over the top. The soft tuff slowly eroded, but caps of harder basalt protected the rock beneath, forming spires.

People have been carving homes and places of worship into the spires for thousands of years.

The Tuff Towns

As long ago as the 6th century BCE, the inhabitants of central Italy built towns and villages on top of steep hills of tuff to protect themselves from attack. Over the years, the buildings and streets continued to be constructed from blocks of tuff, while cellars, tunnels, and underground burial places were carved into the rock below.

Pitigliano is one of Italy's tuff towns, built right on the edge of a cliff of tuff.

DID YOU KNOW? Underground cities big enough to house 20,000 people were carved into the tuff of central Turkey.

Andesite

Andesite is formed from quickly cooling lava that flows from steep-sided stratovolcanoes. There is a long line of andesite volcanoes in South America's Andes Mountains. In fact, andesite gets its name from these mountains.

Volcanoes of the Andes

Andesite is usually formed at convergent plate boundaries, where one plate is moving under, or subducting, another. This makes rock melt, forming magma chambers filled with andesitic magma. When the magma erupts, it cools into andesite. This is how the many volcanoes in the Andean Volcanic Belt were formed, as the Nazca and Antarctic Plates slide under the South American Plate.

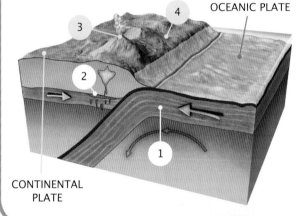

SUBDUCTION ZONES

Subduction zones create volcanic belts and mountain ranges.

OCEANIC PLATE

CONTINENTAL PLATE

1. A heavy oceanic plate slides beneath a lighter continental plate.

2. Rock melts, forming magma chambers.

3. Lava erupts, building volcanoes along a volcanic belt.

4. The continental plate folds and breaks under pressure, forming a mountain range like the Andes Mountains.

Phantom Ship

Phantom Ship is a small island of andesite that pokes above the waters of Crater Lake, Oregon, USA. The island gets its name because it looks like an abandoned sailing ship. Crater Lake is a flooded caldera, formed when the volcano Mount Mazama collapsed 7,700 years ago. A caldera is a huge crater made when a volcano's magma chamber empties, making the mountain above fall inward.

The andesite rock of Phantom Ship is about 400,000 years old.

ANDESITE

Formation: Extrusive

Texture: Aphanitic to porphyritic

Appearance: Gray

Properties: Hard and rough textured

Minerals: Feldspar, plus pyroxene or hornblende

Andesite

The volcano is made of andesite, as well as diorite, the intrusive rock formed when andesitic magma cools underground.

Flamingoes feed in a salt lake. Lakes become salty when the water flowing into them picks up salts and other minerals from the surrounding rock.

DID YOU KNOW? The world's largest Buddhist temple, Borobudur in Java, Indonesia, was built from more than 1.5 million blocks of andesite.

Rhyolite

This photograph of a rhyolite lava dome inside the caldera of Chaitén volcano was taken in 2009.

Rhyolite forms from very thick lava, but eruptions of rhyolite are quite rare. There have been only three rhyolite eruptions in the last century: at Chaitén, in Chile; Novarupta, in Alaska; and St Andrew Strait, in Papua New Guinea.

Growing Treasures

As rhyolite cools, pockets of gas can be trapped in the rock, forming holes called vugs. Later, mineral crystals can grow in the vugs, including gems such as agate, beryl, opal, and topaz. Sometimes, gold forms in deep cracks in rhyolite.

In 1904, gold was found in the rhyolite of Nevada, USA. The town of Rhyolite was founded as miners rushed to the area. When the gold ran out, the town was abandoned.

RHYOLITE

Formation: Extrusive

Texture: Aphanitic or porphyritic

Appearance: Pink or gray

Properties: Vuggy, often containing gems

Minerals: Quartz, sanidine, and feldspar

Rhyolite

The volcano's caldera
is 3 km (2 miles) wide.

Lava Domes

Since rhyolitic lava is thick, it flows very slowly. This means that cooling lava can pile up around a vent, forming a dome shape. Lava domes can be very dangerous. As lava builds up inside, domes can suddenly explode, showering the area in rock, hot gas, and lava.

DOME FORMATION

Lava domes form in the crater of a stratovolcano or around vents in the sides of a volcano.

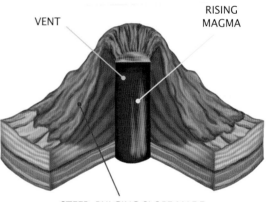

VENT

RISING MAGMA

STEEP, BULGING SLOPE MADE FROM THICK, COOLED LAVA

Dome collapses have caused explosions of ash and gas that force local people to evacuate.

DID YOU KNOW? The largest volcanic eruption of the 20th century took place at Novarupta, Alaska, in 1912, forming a rhyolite lava dome 360 m (1,180 ft) wide.

45

Making Sedimentary Rocks

The Grand Canyon, in Arizona, USA, was carved by the Colorado River within the last 5 or 6 million years.

Most sedimentary rocks form after sediments—bits of rock or the remains of living things—are deposited on the floor of oceans, seas, and lakes. Over thousands or millions of years, the sediment is buried and pressed until it hardens into rock. "Chemical" sedimentary rocks are made from particles of minerals floating in water.

Sorts of Sediment

Sediment can be inorganic (meaning "not from living things") or organic (meaning "from living things"). Inorganic sediment is pebbles, sand, and particles of rock and mineral that are worn away from rocks by weathering, then carried along by rivers, rain, ice, wind, or rock falls. Organic sediment includes dead plants, as well as the skeletons and shells of animals.

TURNING TO ROCK

Sediment is turned to rock through deposition and cementation.

1. **Deposition:** Inorganic or organic particles are deposited, or dropped, at the bottom of bodies of water.

2. **Cementation:** Sediment slowly hardens as it is pressed beneath layers of new sediment. Minerals in the water bridge the gaps between grains of sediment, sticking them together like cement.

SEDIMENTARY ROCK TYPES

Clastic: Formed from inorganic sediment from weathered rocks, with separate grains and pebbles usually visible, and occasional fossils

Organic: Formed from the remains of plants and animals, with fossils and shell fragments sometimes visible

Chemical: Formed from the build-up of minerals dissolved in water, often with a texture of interlocking crystals

Siltstone, a clastic rock with fine grains

DID YOU KNOW? The oldest layers of rock at the bottom of the Grand Canyon are 1.8 billion years old, while the rocks at the rim are just 270 million years old.

Chemical Rocks

Chemical sedimentary rocks form when water has lots of tiny particles of minerals floating around (or dissolved) in it. The mineral molecules start to join together, slowly forming rocks. This can happen quite quickly when the water is evaporating, or turning to gas, leaving the mineral molecules behind.

These "desert roses" are chemical rocks made from sand and mineral particles that formed crystals during the evaporation of a desert pool.

Layers of different sedimentary rocks, including sandstone, shale, and limestone, were formed by different sediments deposited here over millions of years.

Many of the rock layers formed when the region was covered by a shallow sea, but over time the area has also been a beach and a swamp.

Sandstone

China's Zhangye Danxia park is famous for its rainbow layers of sandstone. They formed over 24 million years from different colors of sand and mineral.

Sandstone is made from sand-sized grains of rock and mineral that have been deposited at the bottom of a river, lake, or sea. Sometimes, sandstone forms in deserts, at the bottom of immense sand dunes that are made wet by water seeping up from the ground. Over thousands of years, minerals in the water cement the sand grains together.

Rose-Red Petra

The city of Petra, in the desert of Jordan, was carved from sandstone cliffs about 2,000 years ago. This sandstone is ideal for carving, as it is easy to cut but fairly strong. However, the ancient site has been badly eroded by flooding, rain, and wind.

Petra's Al-Khazneh ("The Treasury") was actually built as a mausoleum, or burial place, for the Nabatean king Aretas IV.

SANDSTONE

Formation: Clastic

Texture: Sand-sized grains

Appearance: White, yellow, brown, pink, red, or black

Properties: Porous, rough, and easy to carve

Minerals: Quartz and feldspar

Sandstone

DID YOU KNOW? Some grains of sand have been cemented into rock, then weathered back into sand as many as 10 times already.

The layers were originally horizontal, but have been tilted by movements in the Earth's crust.

Eroded Arches

Sandstone is quite easily eroded. If the conditions are just right, it can be shaped into arches. These form when water seeps into a crack in the middle of an exposed block of sandstone. When the water freezes into ice and expands, the surrounding rock begins to crumble. The wind blows away loose grains.

Arches National Park, in Utah, USA, has more than 2,000 sandstone arches.

Shale

This rock is made from mud, which is a mixture of water and particles of minerals. Mud is often deposited by slow-moving water, in lakes or at the mouths of rivers. If the mud is buried, after thousands of years the result will be shale.

A Layered Rock

Many thin, flat layers can be seen in shale. This structure, called lamination, is caused by mud being deposited in layers. Then, as the particles of mud are pressed together, they line up quite neatly with each other. Shale can easily be split along these layers.

Oil and Gas

Sometimes dead plants and animals get stuck in mud as it is deposited. As this organic material is deeply buried, it can be heated and pressed until it breaks down into oil and natural gas, which are fuels. Hydraulic fracturing, often called fracking, is a method of forcing the fuel out of the shale.

The layers in shale can be seen clearly on the island of Tung Ping Chau, Hong Kong, where the rock has been battered and broken by waves.

FRACKING

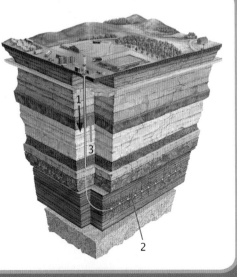

1. A well is drilled down to a layer of shale.

2. A mixture of water, chemicals, and sand is pumped down to the shale, creating cracks in the rock.

3. The sand holds the cracks open as gas and oil are sucked up through the well.

The Burgess Shale region, in the Rocky Mountains of Canada, is famous for the many fossils of ancient sea creatures found there.

SHALE

Formation: Clastic

Texture: Fine grains and thin layers

Appearance: Usually gray or black

Properties: Fissile (breaks easily into flat layers) and may hold oil and natural gas

Minerals: Clay minerals (such as kaolinite and illite) plus quartz

Shale containing a fern fossil

This trilobite, which lived about 505 million years ago, was probably crawling over the seabed in search of food when it died.

DID YOU KNOW? Many people worry about fracking because it can cause small earthquakes, even far from the edge of a tectonic plate, as in the United Kingdom.

Claystone

Claystone is hardened clay, which is a squeezable sort of mud. The rock forms in a similar way to shale, which is also made of mud, but claystone has a different texture because of its different minerals. Unlike shale, claystone does not have thin layers.

Shaping Clay

The minerals in clay, such as kaolinite and illite, form only where there is plenty of water. Molecules of clay minerals contain water. The shape of these molecules, as well as their tiny size, makes them stick to each other but able to move. This makes wet clay easy to shape.

When clay is wet, it can be shaped into pots, bowls, vases, and statues.

The landscape of Zabriskie Point, in California, USA, is made of claystone and other sedimentary rocks that formed at the bottom of a lake which once covered the area.

When rain does fall in this desert region, it cannot soak into the dried-out ground. Streams rush down the hillsides, eroding rills (channels) and gullies (narrow valleys with steep sides).

Firing Clay

When clay dries out, it becomes firm. If dried clay is baked, or "fired," it gets even firmer. Firing makes the clay molecules stick to each other permanently. Fired clay, often called pottery, can last for thousands of years, unless it is accidentally smashed. Historians have learned a lot about the past from examining ancient pottery, from cooking pots to statues of gods.

This cliff is known as the Red Cathedral, because of the rusty shade of its iron-rich rocks.

More than 8,000 pottery warriors were buried alongside the Chinese emperor Qin Shi Huang in 210-209 BCE. He believed they would protect him in the afterlife.

CLAYSTONE

Formation: Clastic

Texture: Very fine grains

Appearance: Pale gray to red

Properties: Quite soft and impermeable (does not let water flow through)

Minerals: Kaolinite, illite, and other clay minerals

Claystone

DID YOU KNOW? Zabriskie Point is named after Christian Brevoort Zabriskie (1864-1936), who ran the local mining of borax, a mineral used in cleaning products.

53

Conglomerate

Conglomerate is made after rounded pebbles, which are heavier than smaller sediments, are deposited by a swiftly flowing stream, glacier, or strong waves. Sand or mud is deposited later, slipping between the pebbles. Eventually, a rock is formed of pebbles surrounded by finer material, called a "matrix."

Puddingstone

Conglomerate rocks are often called puddingstone, because they look like a fruit pudding, with pebble "raisins" in a "cake" matrix! The pebbles make conglomerates difficult to cut cleanly and quite weak, so they are not often used in construction. However, around Boston, USA, the local conglomerate, called Roxbury puddingstone, has been heated and crushed underground, making it a metamorphic rock hard enough to build with.

Roxbury puddingstone was used to construct many buildings in Boston, including the Church of the Covenant.

Breccia

Breccia is similar to conglomerate, but it contains sharp-edged chunks of rock rather than rounded pebbles. Pebbles are eroded into a round shape by being bounced around over time. The sharper chunks in breccia were deposited before they had time to erode.

This ancient Egyptian statue of the goddess Taweret was carved from breccia. She is a combination of hippo, lion, and crocodile.

This conglomerate, in the Carpathian Mountains, Romania, is made of rounded pebbles in a sandstone matrix. It formed on the seafloor, where waves dumped sand and pebbles.

After being lifted to the surface, the conglomerate was eroded into spires.

CONGLOMERATE

Formation: Clastic

Texture: Rounded pebbles surrounded by finer grains

Appearance: Many shades of pebbles and matrix

Properties: Cannot be cleanly cut and has variable strength

Minerals: Depends on the pebbles and matrix

Conglomerate

DID YOU KNOW? In Hertfordshire, England, people used to believe that wearing the local puddingstone could protect against witches.

Limestone

In China, the Guilin region is known for its limestone karst landscape.

Most limestones are organic sedimentary rocks that form from the build-up of shells and coral skeletons on the ocean floor. These animals built their shells and skeletons with the mineral calcite, which is the main ingredient in limestone. A few limestones are chemical sedimentary rocks (see page 64).

Dissolving Away

When limestone comes into contact with rainwater, which is slightly acidic, it slowly dissolves. This means that particles of limestone float away with the water. Over time, this can erode extraordinary features, such as gorges and caves. Landscapes that have been eroded in this way are called karst landscapes.

KARST LANDSCAPES

1. A stream seeps into cracks, eroding a sinkhole.

2. Rainwater soaks into the ground, eroding caves

3. Limestone sidewalks can form at the surface.

LIMESTONE

Formation: Organic

Texture: From tiny grains to bits of shell

Appearance: Pale, from white to light brown

Properties: Hard, dissolves in rainwater, may contain fossils

Minerals: Calcite and aragonite

Limestone

Sidewalks

Sometimes rain can erode limestone until it looks like slabs of stone on a sidewalk. This happens where a layer of limestone has been scraped clear of soil by a glacier that long ago melted. Joints and cracks in the limestone are eroded into wider "grikes."

The flat slabs of limestone are called "clints," which probably comes from the Old English word for cliff ("klint").

Steep towers of limestone, as tall as 300 m (980 ft), have been eroded over millions of years.

Traditional fishermen use trained cormorants to dive into the Li River to catch fish.

DID YOU KNOW? With 651.8 km (405 miles) of passageways, Mammoth Cave in Kentucky, USA, is the world's longest limestone cave.

Dolostone

This rock forms in a similar way to limestone, from the remains of sea creatures. However, once the skeletons have been deposited, they are soaked by groundwater that contains lots of the element magnesium. This changes calcite into the tougher mineral dolomite.

The hoodoos (spires of rock) at Bryce Canyon, USA, were formed by erosion from streams and weathering by ice, which widened vertical cracks in the rock.

Stalactites and Stalagmites

Although dolostone is harder than limestone, it can also be dissolved by rainwater. In dolostone or limestone caves, stalactites and stalagmites can grow. Stalactites form when water, containing dissolved dolomite or calcite minerals, drips from the cave ceiling. The drips leave behind particles of mineral, which grow into icicles of rock. Stalagmites grow up from the cave floor, in pools of mineral-rich dripped water.

These stalactites are in Newdegate Cave, a dolomite cave in Tasmania, Australia.

DOLOSTONE

Formation: Organic

Texture: From tiny grains to bits of shell

Appearance: Pale, from white to light brown

Properties: Very tough, dissolves slowly in rainwater, may contain fossils

Minerals: Dolomite

Dolostone with a trilobite fossil

DID YOU KNOW? The fastest stalactites, with a constant supply of dripping water, grow at 3 mm (0.12 inches) per year.

The top layer is dolostone, which protects the softer sedimentary rocks beneath.

The Niagara Falls

The Niagara Falls are three waterfalls on the border between Canada and the United States. The falls were formed as the Niagara River eroded its path. The top layer of rock is tough dolostone, which eroded much more slowly than the softer shale beneath. As its supporting layer gave way, the dolostone collapsed in chunks. Eventually, this created the three falls.

With a drop of 51 m (167 ft) and a width of 820 m (2,700 ft), Horseshoe Falls are the largest of the Niagara Falls.

Chalk

Chalk is a type of limestone made from the shells of sea creatures called coccoliths and foraminifera. Too small to be seen without a microscope, these creatures are so simple they have just one cell (human beings have trillions of cells).

Chalk Cliffs

Chalk cliffs are common on the coastlines of northern Europe. Since chalk is a very soft rock, the constant battering by sea waves can erode chalk, as well as other soft sedimentary rocks, into extraordinary shapes.

Layers of chalk, deposited at different times, can be seen in the cliffs at Étretat, in France.

COASTAL EROSION

1. **Crack:** The waves erode a crack.

2. **Cave:** The crack grows into a cave.

3. **Arch:** The cave breaks through the headland, forming an arch.

4. **Stack:** The top of an arch collapses, leaving a stack.

5. **Stump:** The stack is eroded into a stump.

DID YOU KNOW? For hundreds of years, chalk was used for writing on blackboards, but today sticks of "chalk" are made in a factory from gypsum.

CHALK

Formation: Organic

Texture: Fine grains

Appearance: White or very pale gray

Properties: Soft, porous, permeable, and may contain fossils

Minerals: Calcite

Chalk

Mushroom Rocks

Mushroom rocks are created when soft rocks are eroded by wind, often in deserts where sandstorms whip up rough particles of sand. The mushroom shape is caused because the wind is stronger—and carries more sand grains—closer to the ground.

This mushroom rock is in Egypt's White Desert, where sandstorms have eroded many chalk features.

This eroded arch is called the Porte d'Aval ("Aval's Door").

Around 71 m (233 ft) high, the pointed stack is known as L'Aguille ("The Needle").

Coal

This valuable rock is made from dead plants, a process that takes millions of years. Coal is called a fossil fuel because it is made from ancient living things—and because it can be burned to produce heat and power.

Buried Energy

The ancient plants that made coal contained energy. They had made it by photosynthesis, the process through which green plants change light energy from the Sun into food energy so they can live. When the plants died, the conditions were just right to prevent the energy from disappearing: it was stored in the coal. We can release the energy by burning coal.

To mine coal deep underground, shafts are dug down to the seam, then slicing and boring machines tunnel into the rock.

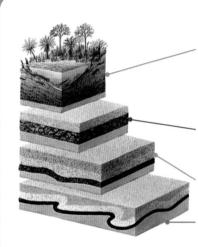

MAKING COAL

1. The process that formed today's coal began 360–300 million years ago, when dead plants sank into a swamp.

2. The decaying plants were covered by sediment.

3. They were pressed and heated.

4. A layer, or "seam," of coal was made.

Problems with Coal

One of the problems with coal is that, since it takes millions of years to form, our supplies of the rock will run out within the next century. Another problem is that when coal is burned it releases the gas carbon dioxide. This traps the Sun's heat in Earth's atmosphere and is contributing to global warming.

Seams of coal are usually deep underground, but sometimes one is pushed close to the surface by plate movements.

Although machinery has made mining much less dangerous than in the past, roof collapses and explosions still put miners' lives at risk.

COAL

Formation: Organic

Texture: From fine grains to plant flakes

Appearance: Black to dark brown

Properties: Can be burned to produce heat, which can be used in power stations to make electricity

Minerals: The element carbon, plus minerals including quartz

Coal

DID YOU KNOW? The earliest known use of coal as a fuel was probably in China, around 5,500 years ago.

Oolite

Oolite (meaning "egg stone") is the name for any chemical sedimentary rock that is formed from tiny round grains, called ooids. These "eggs" build up slowly in water that contains lots of dissolved minerals. The most common oolite is oolitic limestone.

Making Eggs

Ooids can form in warm, shallow water that is full of mineral particles, such as calcite, which forms limestone. Pieces of shell or sand act as "seeds." These seeds are washed around on the seabed, picking up particles of calcite from the water. The ooids can grow until they join together, forming a layer of limestone.

St Paul's Cathedral, in London, England, is built from oolitic limestone, which consists of tiny "eggs" of calcite.

The island of Key West, off the coast of Florida, USA, is made of oolitic limestone.

DID YOU KNOW? Ooids range from 0.25 to 2 mm (0.01–0.08 in) across. Rocks with bigger ooids are called pisolites.

Durdle Door

Durdle Door, in southern England, is an oolitic limestone arch. The limestone formed on the seafloor, but plate movements tilted the layer upright, along with the younger rocks on top. As the sea eroded the coast, the younger, softer rocks farther inland were worn away, leaving a limestone headland. This eroded into an arch.

Around 10,000 years ago, waves eroded an oolitic limestone headland into the Durdle Door arch.

The shallow, warm waters around Key West and nearby islets, including Sunset Key, are popular with tourists.

OOLITIC LIMESTONE

Formation: Chemical

Texture: Tiny spheres

Appearance: Pale, from white to light brown

Properties: Hard, easily carved, may contain fossils

Minerals: Calcite and aragonite

Oolitic limestone under a microscope

Making Metamorphic Rocks

The Black Canyon of the Gunnison is in Colorado, USA.

Metamorphic means "changed in form." Metamorphic rocks are made when any type of rock is changed by great heat or pressure. The resulting rock depends on what sort of rock it was before (called the "parent rock")—and what processes brought about the changes in its make-up and texture.

Contact Metamorphism

There are two main types of metamorphism: contact and regional. Contact metamorphism is when hot magma leaks into solid rock. The surrounding rock is cooked by the heat, but not melted! If the rock melted, it would cool into igneous rock.

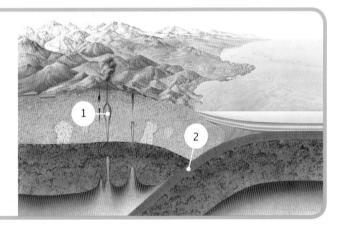

HOW METAMORPHISM HAPPENS

1. **Contact metamorphism:** Magma intrusions heat the surrounding rocks. The closer the rock is to the source of heat, the more it changes.

2. **Regional metamorphism:** The rock is pressed, twisted, and heated by plate movement.

Regional Metamorphism

Regional metamorphism happens over a wider area, or region, than contact metamorphism. Sometimes it happens just because rock is buried deep in the Earth. It is changed by the immense heat and the pressure of all the rock on top. Sometimes it is caused by the movement of tectonic plates, crushing or stretching the rock.

This metamorphic gneiss rock, in Lewis, Scotland, has been pressed so hard that it has folded like a crumpled tissue!

METAMORPHIC ROCK TEXTURES

Foliated: Sheet-like layers (caused by pressure from one side, pushing the mineral crystals into line with each other)

Banded: Layered in different colors (caused by intense sideways pressure, making the crystals line up and sort into types)

Non-foliated: Not layered (caused by being under equal pressure from all sides)

Phyllite, a foliated rock

The streaks of paler rock are dykes of pegmatite, an igneous rock.

The canyon walls are gneiss and schist, which were formed by regional metamorphism about 1.7 billion years ago.

DID YOU KNOW? During metamorphism, the minerals in a rock swap some atoms with each other, forming new minerals—this is called recrystallization.

Quartzite

The parent rock for quartzite is sandstone, in particular sandstone that contains lots of the mineral quartz. Sandstone is changed into quartzite by being heated and crushed where two plates are moving together. This fuses together the quartz crystals, making a very hard rock.

Rock Hard

Quartzite is often formed in fold mountains. It is not easily weathered by rain or eroded by wind and ice. This means that, after softer rocks have been worn away, quartzite is left behind—as ridges, tors, and craggy hilltops.

Known as the "Devil's Chair," this quartzite tor stands on a windswept hilltop in Shropshire, England.

A climber braves a quartzite cliff in the Uinta Mountains of the western USA. The mountains started to form about 65 million years ago.

Shaping Tools

Quartzite has been made into tools for over a million years. A tool-maker would have hit a chunk of quartzite with another rock, causing sharp flakes to fly off. These flakes could be used for cutting, while the quartzite chunk could be shaped into tools for cutting meat, scraping skins, or chopping wood.

A chunk of quartzite is hammered with a rock during tool-making. Do not try this at home, as flakes of quartzite are dangerously sharp!

QUARTZITE

Formation: Regional metamorphism

Texture: Non-foliated with interlocking crystals

Appearance: Usually pale, with other shades caused by impurities

Properties: Extremely hard, slow to weather, and glassy

Minerals: Mostly quartz

Quartzite

DID YOU KNOW? Polished slabs of quartzite are often used as kitchen countertops because they are hard to break, scratch, or stain.

Marble

When limestone is metamorphosed, it becomes marble. Pure limestone turns into white marble. When marble has black, pink, blue, yellow, or green swirls, they were created by impurities in the parent rock, such as bits of clay, sand, iron, or magnesium.

The Taj Mahal, in Agra, India, was ordered in 1632 by the emperor Shah Jahan as a tomb for his most beloved wife.

Changing Limestone

Marble is usually made where two tectonic plates are moving toward each other, crushing a layer of limestone. Sometimes, marble is made by contact metamorphism, when limestone is heated by nearby magma. During metamorphism, the calcite crystals in the limestone grow larger and lock together.

When marble forms, it is often over a wide area and extending far underground. It is carved from the ground in large quarries, such as those at Carrara, Italy.

David

Between 1501 and 1504, the Italian artist Michelangelo carved a block of marble, cut from the quarries at Carrara, into one of the world's most famous sculptures: *David*. Marble is often chosen by sculptors because it is fairly soft and easy to carve but can be polished until smooth. Michelangelo was able to show David's muscles, curls, and expression in fine detail.

In the Bible, David was a young shepherd who found fame by killing the giant Goliath.

DID YOU KNOW? People have been playing "marbles" with little balls of marble and other rocks, clay, or glass for at least 4,000 years.

MARBLE

Formation: Usually regional, sometimes contact metamorphism

Texture: Non-foliated with interlocking crystals

Appearance: White, but impurities create swirls in many colors

Properties: Quite soft, easy to carve, and becomes shiny when polished

Minerals: Usually calcite, plus clay minerals, mica, pyrite, quartz, and graphite

Marble

The onion-shaped dome, which bulges at its base, is 35 m (115 ft) high.

A team of 1,000 elephants hauled the marble blocks from quarries 360 km (220 miles) away.

Hornfels

Hornfels, meaning "horn stone" in German, gets its name from its toughness and texture, which are like animal horn. Hornfels is the name for any extremely hard metamorphic rock that has been baked by the heat from nearby magma. Parent rocks range from shale to basalt.

Musical Stone

The texture of hornfels, with tiny grains packed together like a sidewalk, gives it an odd property: when a slice of hornfels is struck, it rings out! Hornfels from the Skiddaw mountain, in northern England, is traditionally carved into lithophones, or musical instruments made of rock.

The Till Family "rock band" (Daniel Junior, William, and Daniel Senior) play a xylophone made from Skiddaw hornfels in the 1870s.

Cross Stone

Chiastolite, meaning "cross stone," is found in hornfels and other metamorphic rocks that form at high temperatures. Chiastolite is a variety of the mineral andalusite that contains a cross of the dark mineral graphite. As the andalusite crystal grows during metamorphism, it pushes aside particles of graphite, which collect into a regular pattern.

Although stripes of different parent rocks can be seen, the hornfels is too tough to split along these bands.

Some people wear chiastolite as amulets, which are ornaments that are believed to protect the wearer from bad luck.

DID YOU KNOW? Hornfels was traditionally used as a whetstone for grinding the edges of cutting tools to sharpen them.

The hornfels cliffs of Susa, Japan, are formed from layers of sandstone and shale that were baked hard by magma.

This hornfels was metamorphosed around 14 million years ago.

HORNFELS

Formation: Contact metamorphism

Texture: Non-foliated with very fine, tight-packed grains

Appearance: Depends on the parent rock

Properties: Very hard, smooth to touch, and musical

Minerals: Contains some minerals formed only at high temperatures, such as andalusite and cordierite

Hornfels

Lapis Lazuli

Thanks to its deep blue shade, lapis lazuli has been valued as a gemstone for thousands of years. Unlike most gemstones, it is a rock rather than a mineral crystal, since it contains a mixture of minerals. It forms as lumps or layers inside marble, when limestone is heated by nearby magma.

Why So Blue?

This rock gets its name from the Latin words meaning "stone" (lapis) and "of the heavens" (lazuli). The rock's gorgeous color comes from the blue mineral lazurite, as well as smaller amounts of royal blue sodalite. Other ingredients include calcite (white) and pyrite (sparkly gold).

Calcite can often be seen as white layers or mottling in lapis lazuli. Grains of pyrite form stripes and speckles.

Polished lapis lazuli

LAPIS LAZULI

Formation: Contact metamorphism

Texture: Non-foliated with fine grains

Appearance: Deep blue, often with bands or speckles of white and gold

Properties: Beautiful, rare, and can be polished smooth

Minerals: Lazurite, plus calcite, pyrite, sodalite, and others

A chunk of lapis lazuli is cut with a circular saw, and will then be shaped into beads or oval-shaped "cabochons" for earrings and necklaces.

A mask prevents the craftsman breathing in mineral dust.

The most expensive lapis lazuli is the purest blue.

The Mask of Tutankhamun

When the Egyptian pharaoh Tutankhamun died in around 1323 BCE, his body was mummified and placed in a tomb in the Valley of the Kings. A mask was placed over the mummy's face to protect the pharaoh's soul from evil spirits. It was made from gold inlaid with gemstones, including lapis lazuli for the eyebrows and eyeliner, and obsidian for the pupils of the eyes.

The lapis lazuli for the Mask of Tutankhamun was brought more than 3,800 km (2,300 miles) from the Sar-i Sang mines in Afghanistan.

DID YOU KNOW? For hundreds of years, lapis lazuli was ground up and used as a pigment, or coloring, in artists' paints.

Soapstone

This rock is so soft it feels like soap! It contains the soft mineral talc, which is used as talcum powder. Soapstone is formed by regional metamorphism from rocks such as dunite, or where super-heated groundwater flows into rock, soaking and baking it.

Softly, Softly

Soapstone's softness makes it easy to carve. It has been used for sculptures and ornaments since the Stone Age. A useful property of soapstone bowls was soon discovered: the rock absorbs heat, then radiates (or releases it) slowly, keeping food warm. When craftspeople learned to work with metal, soapstone was made into molds to shape knives and spearheads from molten metal.

Begun in the 12th century, the Chennakeshava Temple, in India, is decorated with soapstone carvings of Hindu gods, dancers, musicians, and animals.

SOAPSTONE

Formation: Regional metamorphism or metasomatism (altered by hot water)

Texture: Non–foliated with fine grains

Appearance: Gray, brown, greenish, or bluish

Properties: Very soft, easy to carve, and radiates heat slowly

Minerals: Talc, plus chlorite, mica, and others

Soapstone

Scarabs

Soapstone carvings of scarab beetles were popular in ancient Egypt. Scarabs are a type of dung beetle, which—due to their habit of rolling around balls of dung—came to represent the sun god Ra, who rolled the Sun across the sky.

Scarab carvings were worn as amulets or used as seals, which were pressed into the soft clay that closed documents, leaving a unique pattern from their design.

The soapstone statue has a core of concrete and steel to make it stronger.

Completed in 1931, the 38 m/ 125 ft-tall statue of Christ the Redeemer overlooks the city of Rio de Janeiro, in Brazil.

Christ the Redeemer stands on Corcovado mountain, a giant block of exposed granite. Geologists call these blocks bornhardts, nicknamed "sugar loaves" for their shape.

DID YOU KNOW? Native American peoples heated soapstone rocks in the fire, then dropped them into stews to cook them evenly and slowly.

Slate

Slate forms when shale and other mudstones are pressed between two tectonic plates. Slate is an extremely useful rock, because it is fissile—which means it splits easily into flat sheets. Since ancient times, it has been mined from underground and from open quarries.

Pressed into Sheets

As the clay minerals in the shale are heated and pressed, they start to swap atoms, changing into mica minerals. In micas, the atoms arrange themselves in flat sheets. As the tectonic plates continue to press the rock from the sides, the mineral sheets line up at right angles to the movement. This is why slate is vertically foliated.

In the hands of a skilled craftsperson, slate is easily split into flat sheets of an even thickness.

Slate

SLATE

Formation: Regional metamorphism

Texture: Foliated with fine grains

Appearance: Usually gray

Properties: Fissile (splits into sheets) and does not absorb much water

Minerals: Clay minerals (such as kaolinite and illite) and micas

From Tiles to Tools

As well as being fissile, slate absorbs very little moisture, so it is almost waterproof. This has led to its use as roofing tiles and wipeable blackboards. Slate was also used by Inuit peoples for making *ulus*, flat tools for scraping furs and slicing ice for igloos.

In areas where slate is mined, such as the Eifel region of Germany, every roof is tiled with slate.

Slate has been quarried in north Wales for hundreds of years. In the 19th century, the two local quarries employed 6,000 people.

Slabs of slate are used to construct dry-stone walls to divide fields. Blocks of stone are tightly fitted together like a jigsaw, with no mortar to stick them together.

DID YOU KNOW? Slate is used for the tops of pool and billiard tables, so the balls roll straight and true across the flat surface.

Schist

Like slate, schist often forms from shale, but schist is put under greater pressure at a higher temperature. This changes it more dramatically: it has very strong foliation and large, stretched mica crystals that sparkle when they catch the light.

Dark, heavily foliated cliffs of schist line the Alentejo Coast of Portugal.

Under New York

Schist lies close to the surface beneath Midtown and Downtown Manhattan, the two areas of New York City where skyscrapers cluster. Away from these areas, the Manhattan ground is not strong and stable enough to anchor towering skyscrapers.

An outcrop of Manhattan schist, called Rat Rock, can be seen in New York's Central Park. It is named after the rats that used to scurry over it after dark.

Growing Gemstones

There are different types of schist, formed at different temperatures and pressures— and from different parent rocks. Most types of schist are rich in mica minerals. Some contain large crystals of minerals that are valued as gemstones, such as garnets, emeralds, sapphires, and rubies.

This schist is studded with garnets, a gemstone that forms when shale is being metamorphosed by heat and pressure.

SCHIST

Formation: Regional metamorphism

Texture: Foliated with large sheet-like grains

Appearance: Depends on minerals

Properties: Rough, sparkly, and may contain gemstones

Minerals: Usually mica, plus quartz, feldspar, or garnet

Schist

The battering of the waves has eroded the schist, splitting the rock along its layers.

DID YOU KNOW? Manhattan schist was formed 450 million years ago as two continents came together to form a supercontinent, which geologists call Pangaea.

81

Gneiss

Gneiss (pronounced "nice") forms when granite or sedimentary rocks like shale are intensely crushed and heated as plates grind into each other. Gneiss is defined not by containing particular minerals but by the fact that its different minerals have separated into bands.

Mountain Rock

The plate collisions that form gneiss also build mountain ranges. Gneiss tends to form deep beneath mountains, but—millions of years later—can be exposed at the surface after erosion has done its work. Unlike slate and schist, gneiss does not break along its bands, because some of its minerals are not lined up with each other. It usually erodes quite slowly, sometimes forming craggy outcrops.

The standing stones at Callanish, on the Scottish island of Lewis, were erected between 2900 and 2600 BCE.

A climber conquers a gneiss outcrop in the Swiss Alps.

GNEISS

Formation: Regional metamorphism

Texture: Banded

Appearance: Stripes of different colors

Properties: Rough, hard, and slow to weather

Minerals: Variable, but often has bands of feldspar and quartz

Gneiss containing pink feldspar, gray quartz, and black biotite

DID YOU KNOW? One of the world's oldest known rocks is a gneiss outcrop in Northwest Territories, Canada, which metamorphosed 3.5–4 billion years ago.

The central 13 gneiss stones form a circle, which is surrounded by stones making a cross shape. It is thought that religious ceremonies took place here.

The Troll Wall

The Trollveggen, meaning "Troll Wall," is a cliff of gneiss in Norway. Although popular with brave climbers, dangerous rockfalls are common here. According to legend, the cliff is made of trolls, the cruel, monstrous beings who once lived here. The angry gods turned the trolls to stone as a punishment for their unkindness.

At 1,100 m (3,600 ft) tall, the Troll Wall is the tallest vertical rock face in Europe.

Melted Mix-Ups

Some rocks are not easily put into a group, because they are a mix of metamorphic, igneous, and sedimentary material. They form in strange and sometimes sudden ways! Studying them tells us a lot about the rock cycle—and the forces that have formed our planet.

Migmatites

Migmatite means "mixed rock." Migmatites are usually metamorphic rocks, often gneiss, that have bands or trickles of igneous rock running through them. This happens when a metamorphic rock is heated so it partly melts into magma, because some of its minerals melt at a lower temperature than others. When the magma cools, it forms igneous rock.

This outcrop at Sea Point, in South Africa, is an "injection" migmatite, formed when magma poked its way into sedimentary rocks.

The paler rock in this Antarctic cliff is igneous rock, granite, while the darker rock is metamorphic rock, gneiss.

MIGMATITE

Formation: Usually extreme regional metamorphism, causing partial melting

Texture: Igneous areas have visible grains

Appearance: Pale trickles (leucosomes) in dark rock (melanosomes)

Properties: Hard and slow to erode

Minerals: Leucosomes contain quartz and feldspar, melanosomes contain amphibole and biotite

Migmatite

DID YOU KNOW? If sand is blasted and melted in an impact event, it cools into a transparent glass–like material called impact glass.

Impactites

Impactites are rocks formed during an impact, when a meteorite (or space rock) hurtles into Earth. The shock, pressure, and heat creates rocks that are a mix of melted rock (igneous), changed rock (metamorphic), and shattered rock (sedimentary).

This 1,200 m/3,900 ft-wide crater in Arizona, USA, was made when a meteorite crashed into Earth 50,000 years ago.

Under a microscope, we can see the complex make-up of the impactite called suevite.

The injection of hot magma stretched and changed the sedimentary rocks, so sections of pale granite, dark sandstone, and mixed-up migmatite can be seen.

Body Fossils

A fossil is the preserved remains of an animal or plant from thousands or millions of years ago. A "body fossil" is animal or plant parts that have been preserved in rock. Sometimes, the body parts themselves have turned to rock, but sometimes we find just an outline or an animal-shaped hole.

How Fossils Are Made

Normally, when an animal or plant dies, it rots away. However, if its body is quickly covered with sand or mud, it can be fossilized. Soft parts, such as flesh, usually rot—leaving bone, teeth, and shell. The sediment around the body slowly hardens into rock. Groundwater seeps into the body and dissolves it, but minerals in the water can fill the space, forming a rock copy.

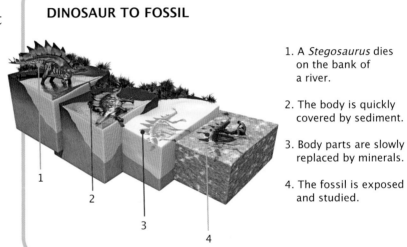

DINOSAUR TO FOSSIL

1. A *Stegosaurus* dies on the bank of a river.

2. The body is quickly covered by sediment.

3. Body parts are slowly replaced by minerals.

4. The fossil is exposed and studied.

Studying the Past

Paleontologists are scientists who study fossils. Since all living things have evolved, or changed, over millions of years, fossils tell us what animal and plant species looked like long ago. A species is a group of living things that look similar and can breed with each other. Humans and goldfish are both species.

Paleontologists are good at finding fossils, often in sedimentary rock. They carefully dig them up, photographing and numbering every tiny piece.

This is the fossil of a nothosaur, a reptile that swam in the oceans between 250 and 200 million years ago.

The nothosaur powered through the water with its webbed feet. The skin and muscles of the feet rotted away, but the bones have been preserved.

Scientists have used robots to model how nothosaurs moved. The tail probably helped the reptile to steer.

FOSSIL RECORDS

Oldest fossil: Fossilized stromatolites (rocky mounds built by bacteria), 3.7 billion years old

Largest animal fossil: The dinosaur *Argentinosaurus*, 39.7 m (130 ft) long and 7 m (23 ft) tall, which would have weighed 70 tonnes (77 tons) when alive

Smallest animal fossil: 50-million-year-old mite on a fossilized spider, 170 millionths of a meter (4 millionths of an inch)

Stromatolites are still formed in lagoons in Australasia.

DID YOU KNOW? Before the 19th century, when dinosaurs were identified as extinct reptiles, people thought their bones must have belonged to dragons or giants.

Trace Fossils

Trace fossils are not records of the body parts of animals and plants—they are the traces left behind by ancient living things. This includes fossilized footprints, burrows, root holes, and poop. Studying trace fossils can tell us about the lives of extinct animals and plants, including how they fed, walked, and defended themselves.

Coprolites

Coprolites are fossilized poops! Like other fossils, their original material has been replaced by hard minerals. Even so, paleontologists can work out what dinosaurs and other ancient creatures had eaten for lunch.

Studying dinosaur coprolites for bones and plant remains reveals whether the animal ate meat or plants, but not usually its exact species.

Burrows

Holes or tunnels dug into the soil or seafloor can be preserved if they are buried by sediment. These burrows may have been the animal's home or a quick place to hide. Sometimes they are the result of a creature—such as a snail—eating its way through the ground in search of food.

These are the fossilized burrows of thalassinideans, shrimp-like creatures that lived in the muddy ocean floor around 170 million years ago.

TRACE FOSSIL RECORDS

Largest footprints: Unknown species of sauropod dinosaur, 130 million years old, 1.7 m (5.6 ft) long

Longest coprolite: Unknown species, 20 million years old, 1 m (3.3 ft) long

Longest trackway: *Climactichnides*, a slug-like creature up to 69 cm (2.3 ft) long, 510 million years old, leaving tracks over 3 m (10 ft) long

Footprints of *Chirotherium*, a crocodile-like extinct reptile

These three-toed footprints were made 145–125 million years ago by a large, meat-eating dinosaur called *Siamotyrannus*.

Footprints can tell us about an animal's gait, or how it walked, how long its legs were, and whether its front limbs touched the ground.

The dinosaur walked across wet sand, which dried and hardened before being covered by other sediment.

DID YOU KNOW? The largest bite marks ever found are 17 cm (6.7 in) long and in the tailbone of a plant-eating *Pukyongosaurus* dinosaur, which lived 130 million years ago.

Sea Creatures

Studying the fossils in different layers and ages of rock has enabled scientists to work out when and where life on Earth began. Simple, tiny life forms appeared in the oceans a little over 4 billion years ago. For the next 3.6 billion years, the oceans remained the only home for all Earth's animals.

Fish

Fish are animals without limbs (arms and legs) that breathe by taking oxygen from the water through their gills. Fossils show us that the earliest fish evolved around 530 million years ago. They did not have jaws for biting, so they sucked up tiny creatures instead.

The outline of this ichthyosaur's skin has been preserved, showing it had a dorsal fin to help it steer.

Around 450 million years ago, the first fish with jaws evolved. Fossils show us their bones, spiny fins, and scales.

SEA CREATURE RECORDS

Largest extinct sea reptile: A Shastasaurid ichthyosaur, 206 million years ago, 26 m (85 ft) long

Largest living sea reptile: Saltwater crocodile, 5.5 m (18 ft) long

Largest extinct fish: *Megalodon* shark, 20-2.6 million years ago, 18 m (59 ft) long

Largest living fish: Whale shark, 12.65 m (41.5 ft)

Ichthyosaur

DID YOU KNOW? Until 1938, people knew coelecanth fish only from ancient fossils, but then living coelecanths were spotted off the coast of South Africa.

This ichythyosaur was a reptile that swam in the oceans between 250 and 90 million years ago.

The long jaws were lined with sharp teeth for snapping up fish or shellfish.

Ammonites

Ammonites were a group of mollusks that lived 240–66 million years ago. Mollusks, such as modern snails, have soft bodies, usually protected by a hard shell. Ammonite fossils are so common they are used as "index fossils." This means that, when a particular sort of ammonite fossil is found, paleontologists use it to pinpoint the age of the other fossils in the same layer of rock.

Ammonites' coil-shaped shells were preserved in the seabed. A whole group, or school, has been fossilized here.

Life on Land

Fossils show us that the first animals to crawl out of the water were amphibians. These early amphibians had developed limbs from their fins and lungs to breathe air, but they still had gills and laid eggs in water. They were the ancestors of modern amphibians (such as frogs and newts), reptiles, birds, and mammals—including humans!

Following the Fossil Trail

Fossils show scientists when different animals evolved. The oldest fossil of an amphibian is 340 million years old. The oldest reptile fossil is 315 million years old. Between those dates, fossils show how some amphibians slowly evolved into reptiles, with a dry, scaly skin and the ability to lay eggs on land. Modern reptiles include snakes, lizards, and crocodiles.

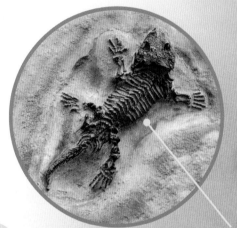

Seymouria, which lived 280–270 million years ago, had features of both amphibians and reptiles. It had dry skin but laid eggs in water.

Mammals

Mammals have hair or fur and feed their young with milk. The oldest mammal fossils are 160 million years old. Mammal fossils need to be identified by their bones and teeth. Fossilized fur is rare and, because they are soft, milk-making glands do not fossilize at all.

Fossils can tell us about mammals that are now extinct, such as mammoths, which died out 4,000 years ago.

LAND MAMMAL RECORDS

Largest extinct: *Paraceratherium*, a hornless rhinoceros, 34–23 million years ago, 15–20 tonnes (16.5–22 tons)

Largest living: African elephant, 2–10 tonnes (2.2–11 tons)

Smallest extinct: *Batodonoides*, an insect-eating shrew, 56–34 million years ago, 0.93–1.8 g (0.03–0.06 oz)

Smallest living: Etruscan shrew, 1.8 g (0.06 oz)

A herd of *Paraceratherium* is preyed on by *Smilodon*.

DID YOU KNOW? In 1975, 140 cave bear skeletons were discovered in a limestone cave in Romania. The animals were probably trapped by a rockfall.

The front legs, which were very strong, were used for holding down large prey, such as camels and bison.

Smilodon was a saber-toothed cat, with extremely long upper canine teeth for killing prey.

This mammal died out around 10,000 years ago, possibly because of climate change or competition from other species.

Meat-Eating Dinosaurs

Around 235 million years ago, a special group of reptiles evolved: the dinosaurs. Around two-thirds of known dinosaurs were plant-eaters (or herbivores), while the rest were meat-eaters (or carnivores). Carnivores had strong jaws, sharp teeth and claws, and ran on their long back legs.

Fossil Clues

Studying fossilized dinosaur bones has revealed how dinosaurs were different from other ancient and modern reptiles. They walked with their legs directly beneath their body, rather than sprawled out to the sides. This helped them to breathe better and move faster.

Fossilized dinosaur eggs tell us that dinosaurs, like most reptiles and birds, made nests for their eggs.

Velociraptor Finds

The first *Velociraptor* fossil was found in 1923. *Velociraptor* was a carnivore that lived 85–70 million years ago. It belonged to the group of theropod dinosaurs, which had hollow, light bones, three-toed feet, and ran fast on their back legs. In 2007, a fossil find revealed that *Velociraptor* had feathers.

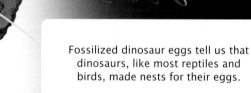

This fossilized skeleton (left) of *Velociraptor mongoliensis* was found in Mongolia, also the home of the herbivore *Protoceratops*, which is shown here winning a battle.

Tyrannosaurus rex's massive jaws were lined with jagged-edged teeth that were up to 30 cm (12 in) long.

The forelimbs were short, but had two strong claws for ripping at prey.

BIGGEST MEAT-EATERS

Spinosaurus: 111-94 million years ago, 15-18 m (49-59 ft) long

Giganotosaurus: 98-97 million years ago, 12-14 m (40-46 ft) long

Tyrannosaurus rex: 68-66 million years ago, 12-13.7 m (40-45 ft) long

Carcharodontosaurus: 100-94 million years ago, 11.9-13 m (39-44 ft) long

Spinosaurus hunted for fish as well as land animals.

DID YOU KNOW? Dinosaurs were named by English paleontologist Sir Richard Owen, using the ancient Greek words for terrible (*deinos*) and lizard (*sauros*).

Plant-Eating Dinosaurs

The earliest dinosaurs were all carnivores that walked on their back legs. Later, plant-eaters appeared, with some species evolving to walk on four legs to better support their weight. Some herbivores developed amazing defenses, from thick plates to horns.

Stegosaurus

Stegosaurus was an armoreded dinosaur that lived 155–150 million years ago. More than 80 *Stegosaurus* fossils have been found in North America and Portugal. This plant-eater had a spiked tail for defending itself, and plates along its back, which may have been used for attracting a mate.

This skeleton, in London's Natural History Museum, is the most complete *Stegosaurus* fossil ever found.

Skulls

Dinosaur skulls can tell us about their lives. Ceratopsids, including *Triceratops*, had sharp horns. These were probably used for defense, but may also have been a way to attract a mate. Pachycephalosaurs had very thick, domed skulls, which were used for head-butting.

Paleontologists are not sure whether *Pachycephalosaurus* head-butted predators or other members of its herd.

Triceratops had three horns and a bony neck frill. The frill may have been for showing off to other dinosaurs in the herd.

BIGGEST PLANT-EATERS

Argentinosaurus: 97–94 million years ago, 30–39.7 m (98–130 ft) long

Alamosaurus: 70–66 million years ago, 30–39 m (98–128 ft) long

Patagotitan: 102 million years ago, 33.5–37 m (110–121 ft) long

Supersaurus: 153 million years ago, 32.5–35 m (107–115 ft) long

Argentinosaurus

This young Apatosaurus stood just under 1 m (3 ft) high.

Fully grown *Apatosauruses* were 22 m (72 ft) long. Long-necked, thick-legged sauropods like *Apatosaurus* were the largest creatures ever to walk the Earth.

DID YOU KNOW? Despite their huge size, fossils show that a sauropod's brain was about the size of a walnut, so they may have been quite simple creatures.

Early Birds

Most dinosaurs died out 66 million years ago, when a meteorite hit the Earth, filling the skies with dust—which blocked out the Sun, killing many plants, plant-eaters, and the meat-eaters that fed on them. Some dinosaurs survived: those that had evolved into birds. Dinosaurs are fluttering outside your window today!

From Limbs to Wings

Over millions of years, a group of light-boned, feathered theropod dinosaurs (see page 94) became smaller and more birdlike. Slowly, the bones of their front limbs changed shape to become wings, with skin flaps and powerful muscles. By 150 million years ago, the dino-bird *Archaeopteryx* was flapping its wings. *Archaeopteryx*, which means "old wing" in ancient Greek, was a halfway point between feathered dinosaurs and modern birds.

Archaeopteryx could not fly well. It probably made short bursts of flight, like modern ground-living birds such as pheasants.

MICRORAPTOR FOSSIL

Microraptor

The dino-bird *Microraptor* lived around 120 million years ago. Unlike modern birds, it had four wings! Fossils tell us that each wing was covered with flight feathers, which are longer and stiffer, giving extra power to help the creature stay in the air.

Scientists analyzed *Microraptor* fossils (above) to determine the color of their feathers. They came to the conclusion they were black!

Fossils show us *Archaeopteryx*'s birdlike features, including its light bones and its wing feathers, seen here as impressions (or dents) in the rock.

Like dinosaurs but unlike modern birds, *Archaeopteryx* had teeth and a long, bony tail.

DINOS TO BIRDS

First dinosaurs with light, hollow bones: Around 220 million years ago

First dinosaurs with tufted feathers: Around 165 million years ago

First short dino–bird flight: Around 150 million years ago

First toothless birds: Around 125 million years ago

Caudipteryx, a birdlike dinosaur that lived 125 million years ago

DID YOU KNOW? Birds survived the catastrophe that wiped out dinosaurs because their smaller size enabled them to adapt better and find enough food.

Ancient Insects

Insects have an exoskeleton (a hard covering), a three-part body, and six legs. The earliest insect fossils are over 400 million years old. As well as being preserved in rock, some ancient insects were preserved in amber, a sticky resin from trees that slowly hardened.

Dragonflies

Dragonflies are one of the most ancient groups of living insects, with fossils as old as 325 million years. The largest insect that ever lived was the *Meganeuropsis permiana* dragonfly, which had a wingspan of 69 cm (27 in).

Pressed into Fossils

Since insects do not have bones, they are not usually fossilized in the same way as large animals like dinosaurs. Some insects left the dents (or impressions) of their bodies as sediments settled and hardened around them. Others were pressed hard in sedimentary rock. Their bodies stained the rock.

Ancient dragonflies, like modern ones, preyed on smaller insects.

This 34-million-year-old wasp's hard exoskeleton stained the shale rock, leaving a record of its form.

Megarachne, a spider-like creature 54 cm (1.8 ft) long

BIGGEST CREEPY-CRAWLIES

Biggest millipede: *Arthropleura*, 315-299 million years ago, 2 m (6.6 ft) long

Biggest scorpion: *Pulmonoscorpius*, 347-331 million years ago, 70 cm (28 in) long

Biggest ant: *Titanomyra*, 50 million years ago, 10 cm (4 in) wingspan

Biggest blood-sucking flea: *Saurophthirus*, 146-100 million years ago, 2.5 cm (1 in) long

DID YOU KNOW? Around 325 million years ago, insects were the earliest creatures to fly, 100 million years before the flying (non-dinosaur) reptiles called pterosaurs.

Amber can be mined from the ground, but is also washed up on the beaches of northern Europe after being eroded from seabed rocks.

This fungus gnat was caught in sticky tree resin around 40 million years ago. The resin hardened and was buried by sediment.

Even the short spines on the gnat's legs have been preserved.

Preserved Plants

Plant fossils can show us what our planet looked like long ago, when the climate was much hotter and wetter or much colder than today. These fossils also give us clues about what animals ate. Some plants have been preserved in rocks, while others have been completely turned to rock, which is known as being "petrified."

Flowers

Fossilized flowers are rare, because petals are delicate and quick to rot. However, some flowers fell among very fine sediments and were gently pressed. Flowering plants evolved around 140 million years ago, but they did not become common until toward the last days of the dinosaurs.

This flower was pressed between fine-grained sediments 35 million years ago.

Cycads

Cycads are called "living fossils" because the modern plants are so similar to ancient fossils. This is unusual, as most ancient species look quite different from modern ones. The oldest cycad fossils are 280 million years old.

Both ancient (left) and modern (right) cycads have large, stiff leaves that do not fall in winter. Cycads do not have flowers: they release their seeds directly to the air on cones.

EVOLUTION OF PLANTS

First land plants: Around 470 million years ago

First plants with roots: Around 407 million years ago

First plants to produce seeds: Around 400 million years ago

First trees: Around 385 million years ago

First flowering plants: Around 140 million years ago

A fossilized fern, which reproduced by releasing spores rather than seeds

This wood was petrified after it was buried under sediment 225 million years ago, then soaked with mineral-rich water. The minerals slowly replaced all the living material in the wood.

These petrified logs are in the Petrified Forest National Park, in Arizona, USA.

DID YOU KNOW? Grass is commonplace today, but the oldest traces of grass—found in dinosaur teeth—are only 113-101 million years old.

Our Ancestors

Modern humans make up the species *Homo sapiens*, which means "wise man" in Latin. *Homo sapiens* have been around for only 315,000 years. Fossils show that our species evolved from a group of apes that lived in Africa about 7 million years ago.

Lucy

In 1974, bits of the fossilized skeleton of one of our ancestors were discovered in Ethiopia. The skeleton belonged to a female member of the species *Australopithecus afarensis*. Nicknamed "Lucy," the girl was 15 or 16 years old when she died, around 3.2 million years ago. Lucy had a small skull like an ape, but walked on two legs, like a human.

Lucy had strong, large jaws for chewing raw plants.

Lucy lived in a family group containing adults and children, males and females.

Scientists have reconstructed what they think Lucy looked like, based on the shape of her skull. Her face looked more like a chimpanzee's than a modern human's.

DID YOU KNOW? At least three other human species—Neanderthal, Denisovan, and Flores—lived at the same time as *Homo sapiens*, but died out by 24,000 years ago.

HUMAN EVOLUTION

Walking on two legs: Around 6 million years ago

Making axes: Around 1.6 million years ago

Controlling fire: Around 1 million years ago

Making shelters: Around 400,000 years ago

Writing: Around 5,000 years ago

Skulls of humans and our ancestors

Laetoli Footprints

Other members of Lucy's species made the world's most famous footprints. The 3.7-million-year-old prints were found in Laetoli, in Tanzania, in 1976. At the time, these were the earliest known footprints showing our ancestors walking on two legs. Today, paleontologists think our ancestors walked upright as long as 6 million years ago.

The footprints were made by two adult *Australopithecus afarensis* as they walked through damp volcanic ash. The Sun baked the ash, before the nearby volcano threw out more.

Although Lucy had a small brain compared to modern humans, she could carve meat with stones she found.

One adult was walking a little behind the other, leaving a trail 24 m (75 ft) long.

Made in the Ground

This crystal of topaz grew in magma as it hardened into rock. It is a semi-precious gemstone known for being transparent.

Minerals are solids that form in the ground or in water. They grow when atoms of different elements join together. Most minerals grow underground, in magma or rock. If the temperature and pressure are just right, the atoms carry on joining in a regular pattern, building a crystal with a symmetrical shape.

Gemstones

Most crystals are only small grains. Together with other crystal grains, they form the mineral mixtures that are rock. But some crystals grow big and beautiful. When beautiful crystals are also hard to break, they are used to decorate rings, necklaces, and art. These crystals are called gemstones.

Gemstones are classed as precious or semi-precious. The rarer and more beautiful gems are "precious." The mineral jadeite is a semi-precious gemstone that is often called jade. It is popular for carvings.

Many Colors

Minerals get their color from the elements they contain. Although some elements often tint minerals a certain color—like manganese, which tends to make pink or purple—a mineral's color is usually the result of the complete mix of elements. A lot of pure minerals, including diamonds, are actually white or colorless, but can be tinted by impurities, or extras.

The mineral sugilite gets its purple color from the element manganese. It also contains other elements, including oxygen, silicon, lithium, and sodium.

Topaz is a mixture of the elements oxygen, silicon, aluminum, fluorine, and hydrogen. Just like a cake, a mineral needs exact quantities of its ingredients.

Uvarovite, a semi-precious mineral

MINERALS AND GEMS

Number of minerals: Around 5,300

Number of precious gemstones: 4 minerals (diamond, emerald, ruby, and sapphire)

Number of semi-precious gemstones: Around 300 minerals, plus over 30 mineraloids (mineral-like solids), rocks, and organic (from living things) substances

DID YOU KNOW? At least 30 possible new minerals are discovered every year, but many of them are decided to be different colors of minerals that are already named.

Made in Water

Some minerals grow in water that has lots of tiny solid particles floating around, or dissolved, in it. The particles start to join together, forming crystals. This is called crystallization. Crystallization often happens as water evaporates, or floats away as gas, leaving the solid particles behind. Minerals formed like this are called evaporites.

Carbonate Minerals

Mineralogists are scientists who study minerals. They divide minerals into groups, depending on their main elements. One large group is the carbonate minerals, which contain carbon and oxygen. Calcite and aragonite are common carbonate minerals that form during a range of natural processes, including evaporation.

These crystals of calcite (left) and aragonite (below) grew in water that contained lots of carbon, oxygen, and calcium atoms.

In Hot Water

Some minerals grow in hot groundwater, which is rainwater that has soaked into the ground and been heated by nearby magma. This water seeps into cracks, or veins, in the rock. Along the way it picks up lots of particles from surrounding rocks. Slowly, the particles crystallize. Minerals formed like this are called hydrothermal minerals, from the ancient Greek words for "hot water."

The hydrothermal mineral fluorite is often found in veins.

MAJOR MINERAL GROUPS

Silicates: Silicon and oxygen, plus other elements
Oxides: Oxygen plus one or more metal elements
Sulfates: Sulfur and oxygen, plus other elements
Sulfides: Sulfur plus a metal element
Carbonates: Carbon and oxygen, plus other elements
Native elements: Only one element
Halides: Fluorine, chlorine, bromine, or iodine, plus a metal element

Sylvite, a halide mineral

DID YOU KNOW? The world's largest crystal was found in the Cave of the Crystals: a 12 m/39-ft long, 4 m/13 ft-wide crystal of gypsum.

These crystals of gypsum formed in the 300-m (980-ft) deep Cave of the Crystals in Mexico.

The cave was once filled with water, heated by a magma chamber beneath. Over 500,000 years, particles of sulfur, oxygen, calcium, and hydrogen crystallized into gypsum.

The cave can no longer be entered, as it has flooded with water again since this photo was taken in 2005.

Crystal Shapes

Mineralogists can often identify minerals by the shape of their crystals. If a crystal has plenty of room to grow, the pattern made by its atoms as they join together, over and over again, gives it a regular shape with a certain number of sides.

Six Families

Perfect crystals are in six main shapes. Mineralogists call these shapes "crystal families."

TRICLINIC
Four-sided blocks with sides of unequal length that are not parallel to each other.

AMAZONITE

MONOCLINIC
Four-sided blocks with a parallelogram base (a four-sided shape with two pairs of parallel sides).

EPIDOTE

ORTHORHOMBIC
Four-sided blocks with a rectangular base (with right angles between the sides).

TANZANITE

TETRAGONAL
Four-sided blocks with a square base (with right angles between the equal sides).

WULFENITE

HEXAGONAL
Rhombohedrons (diamond-shaped "cubes") that may come together in hexagonal (six-sided) shapes.

RHODOCROSITE

CUBIC
Cubes (like dice, with six equal sides).

SPINEL

Crystal Habits

Crystals grow in crowded, changing conditions, so they do not often match the shape of their crystal family perfectly. Some cubic minerals are cube-shaped, but others are flattened into plates, for example. Particular minerals, formed in particular conditions, have the habit of growing in certain ways, such as needles or feathers. These shapes are called their "crystal habit."

The tetragonal mineral rutile has the habit of forming needles. These can grow inside other minerals, such as this quartz.

RAREST MINERALS

Painite: Family: hexagonal; Color: red; Contains: calcium, zirconium, boron, aluminum, oxygen

Alexandrite: Family: orthorhombic; Color: changes in different lights; Contains: beryllium, aluminum, oxygen

Taaffeite: Family: hexagonal; Color: Violet to red; Contains: beryllium, magnesium, aluminum, oxygen

Grandidierite: Family: orthorhombic; Color: turquoise; Contains: magnesium, iron, aluminum, boron, silicon

Alexandrite

Pyrite is a sulfide mineral containing sulfur and iron.

Pyrite belongs to the cubic crystal family, but has a habit of forming more irregular blocky shapes.

The pyrite has grown alongside quartz, a hexagonal mineral with the habit of forming six-sided columns ending in pyramids.

DID YOU KNOW? Pyrite is known as "fool's gold" because its shiny yellow color makes it look like the valuable metal.

Diamond

The mineral diamond contains only one element: carbon. The carbon atoms have formed very strong bonds with each other, which makes diamond one of the hardest natural substances. Pure diamonds are colorless and transparent.

Made in the Mantle

Diamonds usually form right down in the mantle, where the temperature is at least 1,000°C (1,830°F) and the pressure is very intense. The crystals grow in melted material containing carbon. They are brought closer to the surface by deep volcanic eruptions.

Most of the diamonds we have found are over 1 billion years old, but diamonds are still forming in the mantle today.

Diamonds are among the most expensive precious gemstones. Diamonds can be tinted almost any shade by impurities. The most valuable shades are blue and pink, but yellow diamonds are considered poor quality.

DIAMOND

Crystal family: Cubic

Crystal habit: Octahedral (eight-sided)

Appearance: Colorless and transparent, but may be tinted any shade

Group: Native elements

Elements: Carbon

This pink diamond is worth about US$50 million.

DID YOU KNOW? Knives made from diamonds are used in surgery and science to make extremely fine cuts.

Diamonds are cut with many straight sides, called facets. These reflect light inside the gem, increasing its sparkliness.

Every year, people around the world spend more than US$80 billion on diamonds.

The Big Hole

Diamonds are often found in the igneous rock kimberlite, which forms in the mantle but can surge up into the crust in a vertical "pipe." Kimberlite is named after the town of Kimberley in South Africa, which is close to a diamond-rich kimberlite pipe. An open-pit mine, called the Big Hole, was dug into the pipe.

Starting in 1871, 50,000 miners used shovels to dig the Big Hole 240 m (790 ft) into the ground. They found 2,720 kg (6,000 lb) of diamonds.

Quartz

Quartz is a common mineral in Earth's crust, because it is made of the two most common elements there, oxygen and silicon. Most quartz crystals form in cooling magma, but some form in hydrothermal veins. Quartz is part of the mineral mixture of igneous rocks such as granite.

Shaking on Time

Quartz crystals have a useful property: when electricity passes through them, they vibrate (shake back and forth) at a constant speed. Tiny quartz crystals, which vibrate at exactly 32,768 times per second, are used in watches to keep them ticking steadily.

Precious Shades

Pure quartz is colorless and transparent, but the mineral can be tinted many different shades and be translucent (possible to see through, but not clearly) or opaque (not possible to see through). Many of these varieties of quartz are semi-precious gems, including amethyst, which is tinted purple by iron and other impurities.

Although tiny quartz grains are common, large pure crystals are rare and valuable.

Citrine is a yellow to brown variety of quartz, which gets its tint from tiny amounts of iron.

Rose quartz

QUARTZ

Crystal family: Hexagonal
Crystal habit: Six-sided pointed columns, fine grains to large crystals, geodes
Appearance: Colorless and transparent, but may be tinted and translucent to opaque
Group: Silicates
Elements: Silicon and oxygen

Amethyst often forms in geodes. A geode is a hole in the rock that is flooded with hot water and eventually fills with mineral crystals.

This miner is removing the geode by chipping away around the granite surrounding it.

DID YOU KNOW? The first manmade quartz crystal was created in 1845 by copying the natural conditions that grow the mineral.

Corundum

Corundum is an extremely hard mineral, so hard that it is used for polishing and grinding. Pure corundum is quite dull-looking, but it can be tinted any shade by impurities. Beautifully colored, transparent corundums are precious stones. Red corundum is called ruby, while corundum of any other shade is sapphire.

Rubies

Like all varieties of corundum, rubies are made by the heat and pressure as igneous and metamorphic rocks form. They can also be found in sedimentary rocks, after their original rock has been eroded into sediment. Rubies get their color from small amounts of chromium.

This ruby was dug out of metamorphic rock in Tanzania, Africa.

Sapphires

The most well-known color of sapphire is blue, caused by titanium and iron. However, sapphires can be any color other than red. One of the most valuable varieties is the pink-orange padparadscha sapphire. Star sapphires contain needle-like crystals of minerals such as rutile.

A star sapphire shows a six-rayed star pattern.

Many of the world's rubies come from the Mogok Valley in Myanmar, Southeast Asia.

A ruby trader looks through small chunks of marble, eroded by local rivers, to find top-quality rubies that she can sell.

A padparadscha sapphire

CORUNDUM

Crystal family: Hexagonal

Crystal habit: Pyramids, small grains to large crystals

Appearance: Colorless and transparent or translucent, but may be tinted any shade

Group: Oxides

Elements: Aluminum and oxygen

DID YOU KNOW? The largest sapphire found is a blue star sapphire, weighing 280 g (10 oz) and big enough to nearly cover an adult's palm.

Beryl

Beryl often forms in granite, with crystals ranging from tiny grains to some of the most massive ever found. Some varieties of this hard mineral are prized as precious or semi-precious stones. Beryl that is not gemstone quality is sometimes treated to extract the metal beryllium.

These emerald crystals, found in Hunan, China, have formed roughly hexagonal columns.

Not Pure

Pure beryl is colorless, but it can be tinted many colors. In its most precious form, beryl is called emerald, and its green color comes from the mineral chromium. When beryl has traces of iron, it may be semi-precious aquamarine (blue to turquoise), maxixe (deep blue), golden beryl (yellow), or heliodor (greenish yellow). A little manganese makes semi-precious morganite (peach to pink) or red beryl.

This aquamarine has grown next to crystals of dark schorl, another silicate mineral in the hexagonal crystal family.

Morganite on a bed of white cleavelandite

BERYL

Crystal family: Hexagonal

Crystal habit: Columns, pyramids, small grains to massive crystals

Appearance: Colorless and transparent to translucent, but may be tinted green, blue, yellow, and pink

Group: Silicates

Elements: Silicon, oxygen, beryllium, and aluminum

Precious or Semi-Precious

What makes one variety of beryl—emerald— a precious stone, while other varieties are considered semi-precious or not precious at all? It all depends on how many people want to buy a mineral and what they are willing to pay! Large, transparent, nicely tinted crystals of beryl are semi-precious because they are pretty. Emerald is called "precious" because its bright shade makes it more popular—and since it is very rare, people have to pay even more for it.

Most people have not heard of golden beryl, so it sells for a fairly low price, despite its sparkly beauty.

The most expensive emeralds are large, bright green, transparent, and do not have any cracks or inclusions (materials trapped in the crystal during growth).

DID YOU KNOW? When early eyeglasses were made in 13th-century Italy, the lenses were often made of untinted transparent beryl.

Metals

Around 90 elements are metals. When these elements are found in the ground as pure crystals, they are known as native element minerals, because they are minerals that contain just one element. More often, metals are found mixed into minerals with other elements.

Useful Metals

Metals are usually hard, shiny, and easy to shape. These properties make them ideal for tools, machines, construction materials, coins, and art. Most metals let heat and electricity travel through them easily, so they are also used for wiring, electronics, and cooking equipment.

Metal Ores

Most of the metals we use were extracted from ores, which are rocks and minerals that contain large amounts of metal elements. The metal is often removed by smelting, which uses heat and chemicals to break down the ore into its separate parts.

Not many metals are found in the ground as pure crystals, but those that are include copper (pictured), gold, and silver.

These cubic crystals are the mineral galena, which is the main source of the metal lead.

MOST VALUABLE METALS

Rhodium: Used in cars, science, electronics, and jewelry

Platinum: Used in cars, jewelry, medicine, and dentistry

Gold: Used in jewelry, electronics, and industry

Ruthenium: Used in electronics

Iridium: Used in science, medicine, and electronics

Platinum being heated and shaped

Unlike other metals, most gold is found in a pure state.

Gold crystals grow in hydrothermal veins, but grains, flakes, and big nuggets can be picked up in the sediment worn away from rocks and carried along by rivers.

DID YOU KNOW? Metals make up one-quarter of the weight of Earth's crust, with the most common being aluminum, iron, and calcium.

Gems from Living Things

A few gems come from organic, or living, sources rather than being minerals. Some are materials made by living things, such as pearls. Others are fossils, either of ancient living things or the materials they made.

Fossil Gems

Most fossils are not pretty enough to wear on a necklace, and rare fossils should be kept in a museum. However, some pretty fossils are common enough to keep at home. One of these is amber (see pages 100–101), which is fossilized tree resin. Other fossil gems include bones, teeth, and shells that collected hard, sparkling, or bright minerals, such as quartz, as they fossilized.

This gem is fossilized coral. Coral is a hard skeleton made by tiny living things that live in warm, shallow water.

Ammolite is the fossilized shells of *Placenticeras* ammonites. The structure of its aragonite makes it iridescent, or shine in a rainbow of shades.

Living coral

ORGANIC GEMS NOT TO BUY

Coral: Red or pink coral made by living *Corallium* corals, which are at risk from climate change and fishing

Ivory: A hard white material made from the tusks of elephants, which are killed when their tusks are removed

Tortoiseshell: Patterned shells usually from the hawksbill sea turtle, which is in danger of extinction

Jet

Jet is a black gem made of fossilized wood. The ancient wood fell into water, started to decay, then was buried and pressed by sediment. Unlike coal, which forms in a similar way but in thick layers, jet is made from single pieces of wood, which fossilize to become much harder.

Jet pebbles are often found along the coast around Whitby, in northern England. It is carved into earrings, pendants, and beads.

Pearls are made by pearl oysters and mussels when a sand grain or parasite enters their shell. They surround the intruder with layers of nacre.

The shell is also lined with iridescent nacre, often called mother of pearl, a mix of the mineral aragonite with horn-like conchiolin.

DID YOU KNOW? The shells of pearl oysters and mussels are traditionally used to make mother of pearl buttons, jewelry, and keys for musical instruments.

Precious Rocks

Some materials that are valued as gems are rocks rather than minerals, because they contain a mix of different minerals. Other gems are mineraloids, which are solids that look like minerals but have atoms that are not arranged in an ordered pattern.

Tiger's Eye

This yellow-brown rock reflects the light in what seem to be rippling streaks. This chatoyant (from the French for "cat's eye") effect is caused by parallel threads of two silicate minerals forming side by side: quartz and crocidolite.

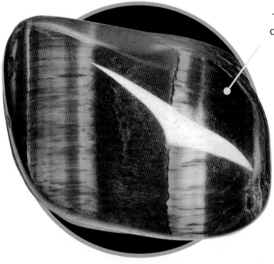

To see the "cat's eye" effect clearly, tiger's eye should be cut into a smooth, domed shape called a cabochon.

Orbicular jasper is jasper that contains orbs (or circles) of different minerals and mineral mixtures.

Jasper

Jasper is an opaque rock that is a mixture of quartz and moganite. Both minerals are made of silicon and oxygen atoms, but in a slightly different structure. Jasper is often tinted by impurities such as iron, which makes it red, and striped or spotted by other minerals. It is carved and polished to make beads, vases, and boxes.

Opal is a mineraloid containing silicon and oxygen atoms, with water molecules caught up inside its structure.

Opal is prized for its iridescence. This is caused by the way the opal's structure bends the light, breaking it up into all its rainbow shades.

VALUABLE ROCK GEMS

Agate: Appearance: translucent, often banded; Contains: quartz and similar minerals

Maw sit sit: Appearance: opaque, green and black; Contains: kosmochlor, jadeite, and feldspar minerals

Tiffany stone: Appearance: opaque, purple and white; Contains: fluorite and quartz minerals plus opal

Unakite: Appearance: Opaque, green and pink; Contains: feldspar, epidote, and quartz minerals

Agate

DID YOU KNOW? Most opals come from the town of Coober Pedy, in Australia, where it is so hot that many miners live in dark caves dug into the hillside.

Glossary

ACIDIC
Able to dissolve some substances.

AMPHIBIAN
An animal that lives in water and breathes through gills when young, but develops lungs for breathing air and can live on land as an adult.

APHANITIC
Describes an igneous rock with mineral crystals too small to be seen with the human eye.

ATOM
The smallest part of any material that can exist on its own.

BACTERIUM (pl. BACTERIA)
A tiny, very simple living thing.

CANYON
A narrow valley with steep sides.

CHEMICAL ROCK
A sedimentary rock made when minerals dissolved in water form crystals.

CLASTIC ROCK
A sedimentary rock made from pieces of rocks and minerals that were broken off by weathering.

COMPOUND
A material made of two or more elements whose atoms are bonded to each other.

CONTACT METAMORPHISM
The process during which a rock's minerals and texture are changed by the heat of nearby magma.

CONTINENTAL PLATE
A tectonic plate that is mostly or completely covered by land.

CONVERGENT BOUNDARY
An area where tectonic plates are moving toward each other.

CRUST
The hard, rocky outer layer of Earth.

CRYSTAL
A solid element or mineral with atoms arranged in a regular pattern, forming a symmetrical shape.

CRYSTAL FAMILY
The geometric shape formed by a crystal's atoms.

CRYSTAL HABIT
The usual form of a particular crystal growing in particular conditions.

DINOSAUR
An animal belonging to a group of extinct land-living reptiles.

DISSOLVE
When small parts of a solid break off and are mixed into a liquid.

DIVERGENT BOUNDARY
An area where tectonic plates are moving away from each other.

DYKE
A sheet of rock inside the body of another rock, often formed by magma flowing into a crack.

ELEMENT
One of 118 substances that cannot be broken down into simpler substances and are the building blocks for everything on Earth.

EROSION
The removal of rock or soil by water, ice, or wind.

EVAPORATE
To change from a liquid into a gas.

EXTRUSIVE ROCK
A type of igneous rock formed when lava cools and hardens on the Earth's surface.

FAULT-BLOCK MOUNTAIN
A mountain formed when large chunks of rock are pushed upward, caused by movements in the crust.

FISSILE
Easily split into layers.

FISSURE VENT
A long crack in the crust through which lava can erupt.

FOLD MOUNTAIN
A mountain formed where tectonic plates are moving toward each other, pressing rock upward.

FOLIATED
With many thin layers.

FOSSIL
The remains or traces of an ancient animal or plant that have been preserved in rock.

GEOLOGY
The science that studies the structure of the Earth and the forces that shape it.

GLACIER
A slowly moving mass of ice formed by the build-up of snow on mountaintops or in cold regions.

GRAVITY
The force that pulls all objects toward each other, with larger objects, such as planets, having a greater pull than small objects.

IGNEOUS ROCK
A rock formed when magma or lava cools and hardens.

IMPURITY
A small amount of another substance that is present in a material.

INORGANIC
Not made from living things.

INTRUSIVE ROCK
A type of igneous rock formed when magma cools and hardens inside the Earth.

LAVA
Hot, molten rock that has erupted from a volcano or fissure vent.

MAGMA
Hot, molten rock inside the Earth.

MANTLE
The rocky layer of the Earth between the super-hot metal core and the cooler, solid crust.

METAMORPHIC ROCK
A rock formed when any rock is put under great heat and pressure, changing its minerals and texture.

METEORITE
A piece of rock or metal that has fallen to Earth from space.

MINERAL
A solid made when atoms of one or more elements join together in a regular, repeating pattern.

MOLECULE
A group of atoms that are joined to each other.

MOMENT MAGNITUDE SCALE
A scale running from 0 to 10 which measures the strength of earthquakes.

OCEANIC PLATE
A tectonic plate that is mostly or completely covered by sea.

OPAQUE
Not able to be seen through.

ORGANIC
Made from living things, such as animals and plants.

OUTCROP
Rock that is exposed at Earth's surface.

PEGMATITIC
Describes an igneous rock with crystals larger than 2.5 cm (1 in).

PERMEABLE
Lets liquids pass through.

PHANERITIC
Describes an igneous rock with crystals large enough to be seen with the human eye.

PLUG
A vertical "pipe" of igneous rock formed when magma cools inside the vent of a volcano.

POROUS
With many holes, letting liquid or gas pass through.

PORPHYRITIC
Describes an igneous rock with both large and small crystals.

PYROCLASTIC
Describes an igneous rock made of fragments thrown from a volcano.

REGIONAL METAMORPHISM
The process during which rocks are changed over a wide area as a result of heat and pressure.

REPTILE
An animal with a dry, scaly skin that lays eggs on land.

ROCK
A solid mix of different minerals.

SEDIMENT
Fragments of rock and mineral broken down by weathering and carried away by erosion.

SEDIMENTARY ROCK
A rock formed from hardened sediment.

SHIELD VOLCANO
A volcano with gently sloping sides.

SPECIES
A group of living things with similar characteristics, which can breed with each other.

STRATOVOLCANO
A tall, steep-sided volcano.

SUBDUCTION ZONE
An area where one tectonic plate is sinking under another.

TECTONIC PLATE
One of the giant, slowly moving chunks of rock that make up the Earth's crust and upper mantle.

TOR
A bare rocky hill or heap of rocks.

TRANSFORM BOUNDARY
An area where tectonic plates are moving sideways past each other.

TRANSLUCENT
Able to be seen through, but not clearly.

TRANSPARENT
Able to be seen through clearly.

WEATHERING
The breakdown of rocks at the Earth's surface by weather, water, and living things.

Index